JAMES R. WILLIAMS is a member of the Department of Economics at McMaster University and the author of *Resources, Tariffs, and Trade: Ontario's Stake.*

This study examines the effect of the Canadian-United States tariff by determining the industrial output and price cost relationships which would exist in its absence and comparing them with actual output levels under present tariff schedules. A general description of the adjustment process in Canada which would occur in free trade is followed by a detailed discussion, including theoretical and empirical analysis, of six sectors: iron and steel, non-ferrous metals and electrical products, wood and paper products, chemical and chemical related industries, textile products, and agriculture and food.

The model adopted in this book is distinctive in that it considers the simultaneous impact of *both* the Canadian and the US tariffs with explicit consideration of the Canadian resource base. Further, it reflects the impact of the tariff on the cost of intermediate goods purchased by each industry, based on their role in trade.

The results indicate that manufacturing in Canada would expand in free trade and that the level of manufacturing would shift toward the end stages of processing. The implications of this analysis will be of interest to professional economists in government and industry in both Canada and the United States.

JAMES R. WILLIAMS

The Canadian-United States tariff and Canadian industry: A multisectoral analysis

UNIVERSITY OF TORONTO PRESS
Toronto Buffalo London

©University of Toronto Press 1978
Toronto Buffalo London
Printed in Canada

Canadian Cataloguing in Publication Data

Williams, James R., 1930-
    The Canadian-United States tariff and Canadian industry

    Bibliography: p.
    Includes index.
    ISBN 0-8020-5355-6

    1. Tariff—Canada. 2. Tariff—United States.
    3. Canada—Industries. I. Title.

    HF1766.W552   382.7'0971   C77-001647-2

To the memory of Lila May Williams

Contents

Preface

Because of the large volume of trade between Canada and the United States, the tariff items in the schedules of both nations are of particular significance to Canadians. The impact of trade barriers on the level of output in specific industries is a subject which has received considerable attention in the technical literature of economics, and a variety of analytical methods has been employed in attempts to improve understanding of the issues. In this book a general equilibrium approach is adopted, which emphasizes the interdependence of all industrial sectors.

Since 1965, stimulated by the pioneering articles of Balassa (1965), Johnson (1965), and Corden (1966), a substantial body of literature has evolved which is now called the theory of effective protection.[1] This literature represents a modification of the general theory of tariffs. In the older literature, intermediate processing was ignored and it was implicitly assumed that each firm was vertically integrated and that tariffs applied only to the end product stage. In the newer approach, it is explicitly recognized that changes in the tariff will affect *all* prices, including the prices of intermediate goods and that, therefore, the relative costs of *all* commodities are changed by a tariff protecting any particular one. The 'effective tariff' is a concept which can take this interdependence into account. Recent literature,[2] however, has demonstrated that there is a need for a more general approach than can be achieved through application of the theory of effective protection alone. In the words of one of the pioneers of the theory (Corden, 1971a, 56), 'One can no longer look at each product, with its tariff and production function, separately and build up a scale of adjusted effective rates which can form the basis for a general equilibrium analysis.'

It should be emphasized that while no approach can be totally general, it is clearly desirable to combine, in a logically consistent manner, as much of the relevant and reliable data as are available. The technique of linear programming provides a natural vehicle for this, and fortunately, there is a well-developed literature on the subject.[3] The approach taken in this study is distinctive in that it explicitly takes account of both the foreign (United States) tariff and the production constraints implied by resource supplies. Earlier studies which applied the linear programming approach to trade problems usually assigned a set of base year capacity levels to each producing sector and, except for the studies by Werin (1968) and Lage (1970), expansion of capacity in each industry was treated as an endogenous variable. If one is willing to assume that the base period technology will hold in the longrun, such an approach can be a useful guide to economic planning.

In this study, however, planning is not the objective and hence the constraints are different. Forty-one resource constraints are specified along with a balance of trade constraint. In all there are sixty-three industries which must compete for these resource supplies. Since economic planning is not an objective of the analysis, expansion of capacity through investment over time is not considered. Interest is focused on the general impact of the tariff rather than on the long-term size of each industry, and capacity is assumed to be expandable, at constant cost, within a range of ten per cent without additional investment. To determine the general equilibrium impact of the tariff, output levels which maximize consumption when the tariffs are at their observed levels are compared to the levels which produce maximum consumption under free trade. Such an approach is ideally suited to a study such as this which attempts to assess the impact of the entire schedule of Canadian and American tariffs.

As noted above, this is the first general equilibrium study which has given consideration to the impact of the foreign tariff. Recent literature (McDougall, 1970; Ray, 1973; Dornbusch, 1974; and Schweinberger, 1975) has demonstrated the need for special treatment of that sector of the economy which does not compete with imports. It has been the author's contention for several years that it is logically necessary to distinguish among firms belonging to *three* sectors: the import competing sector, the domestic sector and, very importantly, the export sector. Unless the export sector is given explicit recognition, the empirical results of research cannot take into account the effect of changes in foreign tariffs, and Canadian trade would be treated as though it were independent of foreign tariffs. Even though this seems invariably to have been the practice in both theoretical and empirical research until now, it must be regarded as a serious omission. Whether an industry (in free trade or under the tariff) should be viewed as belonging to the import competing sector, the domestic sector or the export sector ought not merely to be assumed, but should be determined empirically as it is in this study (where it forms part of the solution to the linear programming problem itself). Simultaneously, this study determines in the 'dual' to the linear programming model, whether the domestic or foreign tariff will play the principle role in setting the Canadian price of a commodity relative to its foreign price. This illustrates the power of linear programming when applied to such problems. In addition to its consistent treatment of domestic prices relative to foreign prices, this approach entails a logically consistent determination of the exchange rate and relative prices in Canada.

The most general conclusions resulting from the study may be summarized as follows: (1) manufacturing would expand in Canada under free trade, and (2) the degree of processing would shift toward end product production. The model, however, is not sufficient by itself for such conclusions unless it is corroborated by other research. With this purpose in mind the author has reviewed other scholarly sources and, in part two, the general equilibrium results are compared to other quantitative evidence. This secondary evidence corroborates the two general conclusions and enhances one's confidence in the results. Confidence in the results of the model, as they apply to any particular one of the sixty-three producing classifications, should also be subject to corroborating evidence of a partial equilibrium kind. The results of the discriminant analysis described in chapter one demonstrate how evidence of a partial equilibrium nature may be used to corroborate such general equilibrium results.

A number of people generously read parts of this book in its various stages. Professor I.F. Pearce, University of Southhampton, and J.C. Leith of the University of Western Ontario read earlier versions of chapter two. D.J. Daly of York, R. Tremblay of the Université de Montréal, and B.W. Wilkinson from the University of Alberta made helpful comments at the Seventh Annual Economic Association meeting in 1974. In addition, several of my colleagues at McMaster, including P.J. George, E.H. Oksanen, A.A. Kubursi, W. Mackenzie, and R.A. Muller, have read various chapters.

Completion of the project required solutions to numerous technical problems. In particular, the model is based on a special tabulation of input-output data and this tabulation was kindly supplied by the Input-Output Research Development Staff at Statistics Canada. I should like to express my appreciation to T. Gigantes and R. Hoffman for their advice and help. When the data arrived at McMaster, I was fortunate to have the excellent research assistance of P. Jacobson and the (then) department computer specialist, Mrs M. Derrah. Research and clerical assistance was made possible by several grants from the Canada Council. This book has been published with the help of grants from the Social Service Federation of Canada, using funds provided by the Canada Council, and from McMaster University.

JAMES R. WILLIAMS
McMaster University

PART ONE

1

Summary and general conclusions

The tariff has been the object of a considerable amount of attention in Canada. Most notable in the literature of recent times is Young's comprehensive study of 1957 and, a decade later, monographs by Eastman and Stykolt (1967) and Wonnacott and Wonnacott (1967). On these latter two, the question of economies of scale is thoroughly reviewed but otherwise the subject matter is differentiated. In Eastman and Stykolt (1967) the problem of market structure predominates, whereas in the research of Wonnacott and Wonnacott, one finds an extensive study of locational factors and their relationship to trade between Canada and the US. It becomes quite clear after reading these manuscripts that very little can be added to what these authors have already achieved and there is no attempt to do so here. This book is concerned with a different but related topic, namely, a study of the Canadian-US tariff in a general equilibrium model.

To trace out the effects of the tariff is an extremely complex task which cannot be accomplished without simplifying assumptions. The assumptions chosen will depend on the research goals to be achieved and clearly there is no single methodology that can predominate over all of the others. In the partial equilibrium approach, it is assumed, that, in addition to the exchange rate, all prices and output levels are fixed except in the firms or industries under consideration. This permits one to study intensively many important relationships at the level of the firm, industry or industrial sector. In a general equilibrium study of the type illustrated by this book, an alternate set of simplifying assumptions are required in order to focus on the inter-relationships between industries. In this book the tariff is studied as a part of an interdependent system in which output levels, relative prices and the exchange rate are simultaneously determined.

The opportunity for such a study was presented when several essential data sources became available for the same year. The 1961 version of the Canadian input-output table is the first of its kind since publication of the 1949 table. The year 1961 is also the date chosen by the Committee for Economic Development for a comparative study of the US and European tariff schedules. As a consequence, the US tariff is available for this date organized according to the Standard International Trade Classification. It therefore became apparent that these data sources could be combined in a general study which might be used as a bench mark for comparisons with research of earlier or future periods. Because it would emphasize the general equilibrium approach, the project might also prove a useful supplement to studies focused on a single firm, industry or sector of the economy.

The foundations for research of this type were laid in the late forties culminating with a significant volume edited by Koopmans (1951). It became quickly apparent after these methods had been established that they could be used to study certain theoretical questions in international trade[1] and this, in turn led to a number of empirical studies in which activity analysis was employed[2] to determine, simultaneously, the effect of the tariff on a broad range of variables including relative output levels and prices. In this book activity analysis is applied in the format of a multisectoral model of the Canadian economy.

The model is described mathematically in chapter two. This chapter is concerned primarily with a verbal account including a discussion of the assumptions required and some suggestions concerning the interpretation of the empirical results. Although the verbal account of the model will be supplemented occasionally by symbolic representation of certain concepts, the discussion in this chapter will avoid the use of mathematical techniques.

A BRIEF NOTE ON LINEAR PROGRAMMING

A considerable part of economic analysis is concerned with the problem of either maximizing or minimizing an objective in the presence of restrictions or constraints. We may refer to this as optimizing behaviour. Linear programming is distinguished by the manner in which one expresses mathematically the objective which is to be optimized and the nature of the restrictions which are imposed. This is illustrated below for the case of the multisectoral model considered in this study. An illustration which may be more familiar to the reader is associated with the theory of the firm. In such an application the problem might consist of maximizing profits subject to constraints imposed by the limited amount of available machine time (of various types of equipment) and by the limited amount of labour (of various types of skill).[3] The processes which use machines and labour are called activities. More specifically, an activity represents a list of requirements including the amount of machine time (for each type of equipment) and the amount of labour (of each type of skill) required to produce one unit of output. The optimization problem is to choose from among many technically possible activities in order to reach the highest possible level of profit, subject to the constraints that the amount of time used for each type of machine and the amount used of each type of labour skill must not exceed the amount available.

Whenever a maximization problem of this type is defined, a minimization problem (called the dual) is also implicitly present. In the case being illustrated, the maximization of profit would be associated with a dual problem in which the cost of fixed resources would be minimized subject to constraints which impose the requirement that no productive activity is to be used if such use entails loss. The maximization problem and the minimization problem are linked together by a fundamental theorem in linear programming which holds that the solution to the maximization problem contains the solution to the minimization problem and conversely. Therefore, in a practical sense, it makes no difference whether optimization is achieved through maximization of profit or minimization of the cost of fixed resources.

In this book a similar application of the theory of linear programming is applied to the national economy depicted as a set of inter-related industries. The main goal is to simulate the behaviour of the economy under conditions of free trade. In the model, output of consumption goods is to be maximized subject to the availability of resources. We assume that the relative proportions of the various commodities consumed by Canadians in 1961 are unchanged. The solution to the maximum problem is obtained first with tariffs in Canada and the US at their observed level and then with these tariffs set at zero in order to obtain the free trade solution. In the former case, the solution must reproduce the observed situation. In the latter case, the solution determines the levels of output, exports and imports necessary to maximize consumption in free trade. The solutions in either case are based upon the assumption (implicit in the dual minimization problem) that firms, faced with the possibility of buying (or selling) at a price higher in Canada or the US will choose to buy (or sell) in the market where the price is lower if the firms are buying (and higher if the firm is selling). The major features of this linear programming format are described in the following section.

THE MULTISECTORAL MODEL

In the multisectoral model, conditions of production are represented by a list of coefficients. Each coefficient indicates the amount of input required per dollar of output in that industry. The first industry might be represented by a vector or activity such as

$$\begin{bmatrix} -1 \\ a_{21} \\ b_{11} \\ b_{21} \\ 0 \end{bmatrix}$$

In this representation, supply is designated by negative numbers and demand by positive numbers. Negative unity appears in the first position indicating that this process represents one unit of output. The next three coefficients are positive numbers because they are inputs demanded by the firm. The coefficient a_{21} represents the amount of industry 2 goods needed as intermediate product to produce one unit of output in industry 2. The coefficient b_{11} in the third position represents the amount of the first resource needed to produce a unit of output in the first industry and b_{21} represents the amount of the second resource needed. A zero appears in the last position indicating that none of this resource is used to produce the output of industry 1. When operated at level x_{01}, this activity produces $-x_{01}$ units of commodity 1 using $a_{21}x_{01}$ units of output of the second industry, $b_{11}x_{01}$ units of resource 1 and $b_{21}x_{01}$ units of resource 2.

Production activities are a source of supply but not the sole source of supply of commodity one. Goods are made available through imports as well. These imports are represented, in the case of goods competing with the output of the first industry, by the vector,

$$\begin{bmatrix} -1 \\ 0 \\ 0 \\ 0 \\ p_{21} \end{bmatrix}$$

Negative unity appears in the first position representing a unit increase in the supply of imports. Zeroes appear in positions 2, 3, and 4 because no inputs of intermediate goods or resources are required to obtain imports. In order to acquire a unit of imports, p_{21} units of foreign exchange are demanded. The coefficient p_{21} is the price of commodity 1 in the currency units of nation 2 which is assumed to be the price in 'the rest of the world.' This appears in the last position of the import vector as a positive number because it is an item of demand. Now it can be clarified why a zero appears in the last place of the production activity vector. This place lists the amount of foreign exchange required by the activity in question and no foreign exchange is used directly in the production of goods. If the import activity is operated at level m_{01}, $-m_{01}$ units of industry 1 goods are added to supply and $p_{21}m_{01}$ units of foreign exchange are demanded.

The foreign exchange needed to acquire imports is earned from export activities which, in the first sector, are represented by the vector

$$\begin{bmatrix} 1 \\ 0 \\ 0 \\ 0 \\ -p_{21} + s_{21} \end{bmatrix}$$

Positive unity appears in the first place representing a unit of export. Zeroes appear in the second, third, and fourth positions because neither intermediate goods nor resources are used up in the process of exporting. In the last position the quantity $(-p_{21} + s_{21})$ appears. As noted above, p_{21} is the foreign price received for exports. From this we deduct s_{21}, the specific tariff in nation 2 on commodity 1. One unit of sector one exports adds $(-p_{21} + s_{21})$ units to the supply of foreign exchange reserves. If e_{01} units of exports are demanded, an amount of foreign exchange equal to $(-p_{21} + s_{21})e_{01}$ is supplied.

There is one final activity in the model which has not yet been described. It may be represented by the vector

$$\begin{bmatrix} w_1 \\ w_2 \\ 0 \\ 0 \\ 0 \end{bmatrix}$$

Here w_1 and w_2 are the amounts of sector 1 goods and sector 2 goods demanded for consumption when this activity is at unit level. Zeroes appear in the third, fourth, and fifth place because neither resources nor foreign exchange are consumed by households. When this activity is at level y, $w_1 y$ units of commodity 1 and $w_2 y$ units of commodity 2 are shipped to households.

The effects of numerous individual decisions operating through the market mechanism will determine the amount of each commodity produced and supplied. In each of the j sectors the activity levels x_{0j}, m_{0j}, and e_{0j} are determined in a way that simulates the actual behaviour of the economy under various assumed conditions. (The mathematically inclined reader may wish to refer to Table 2.2 where a slightly more elaborate version of the model is displayed in table form.) By making various changes in the model one can simulate the actual effects of the tariff and determine, under alternate hypotheses, the output levels, trade and the level of aggregate consumption.

The simulation is concerned with the year 1961. The actual bundle of goods consumed in 1961 is used to define an index of welfare. Weights are determined by dividing the actual amounts of each commodity consumed by households in 1961 by the level of national income in 1961. The weights themselves constitute one unit of what is called the composite commodity. The simulation is based on a linear programming algorithm in which the solution reproduces the actual 1961 situation. The 1961 level of the composite commodity, the levels of output in each industry in 1961 and the actual levels of imports and exports of 1961 are the solution to the primal problem and the actual 1961 prices and exchange rate form the solution for the dual problem. By setting all tariffs and taxes at zero, it is possible to obtain a simulated version of what we call the free trade situation. As will be shown mathematically in chapter two, the largest amount of the composite commodity is obtained in the free trade solution and this, therefore, is used as a norm for assessing the Canadian comparative advantage.

ADVANTAGE OF THE MULTISECTORAL MODEL

Canadian tariffs increase the cost of imports relative to domestic production in Canada. The greater the Canadian tariff the greater the tendency to substitute local production for imports. Canadian exports are imports in the foreign nation of destination. The greater the foreign tariff the greater the tendency in the foreign nation to substitute domestic production for goods imported from Canada. In this obvious way tariffs protect domestic production in all nations and reduce the volume of exports. The matter is much more complicated than this however and it would constitute a source of error if we left matters at this naive level because it would imply that the price-cost relationships in each industry are independent of prices and costs in every other industry.

Tariffs protect individual producers in the market but they cannot protect the economy as a whole because of the balance of trade and resource supply constraints. In order to purchase Canadian exports, foreign nations must sell goods in Canada to acquire Canadian currency. Unless Canada is prepared annually to make unilateral transfers or loans (private or public) to foreign nations, any reduction in imports must be matched dollar for dollar by reduced exports. The tariff can encourage expansion in industries competitive with imports but only by depriving the exporting industries of part of their foreign market and hence some of their potential growth. Furthermore, the export industries and all other industries which are *not* protected must compete with the import competing industries (which are protected) for limited resource supplies. As protected industries expand, they bid away resources and intermediate goods from the export industries and thereby force them to contract relative to import competing industries.

Because of the abundance of natural resources in Canada, relatively more productive effort is devoted to agriculture and mining than is true for most other nations in the world. The Canadian tariff is generally assumed to operate as an offsetting force which shifts the focus of production forward to higher levels of processing. The actual effect of the tariff is a complex question. It is likely that the public does not fully understand the extent to which commercial policy in Canada and to some extent that of the United States favors the relative growth of fishing, agriculture and mining. Like the tariff schedules of most nations, the Canadian tariff offers forms of protection to all sectors and therefore attempts, implicitly, to expand all sectors simultaneously. This is an objective which simply cannot be achieved through tariff policy. It must either fail completely or it will encourage the growth of some industries and discourage production in others. The effect of any particular tariff is diffused throughout all sectors. The simulation is a means of determining which productive activities are encouraged and which are discouraged by the tariff. The levels of output observed in the tariff situation are compared to the levels of output which would be expected in a situation of free trade. The sectors which are actually protected by the tariff are those which are larger when the tariff is present and smaller in free trade.

The multisectoral model brings into consideration many general equilibrium aspects of tariffs which cannot be studied in a partial equilibrium framework. Nevertheless, it is important to bear in mind that no model can reproduce all of the details of reality and many aspects of this topic are best studied in a partial equilibrium framework. As with the partial equilibrium method, simplifying assumptions are needed to reduce the total amount of mathematical description to a computationally manageable size. The assumptions necessary for the multisectoral model are discussed below. The implications of these assumptions are more easily explained, however, if we first divert to a brief discussion of the relationship between the firm and its corresponding industrial sector.

RELATIONSHIP OF FIRMS TO INDUSTRIAL SECTORS

In an activity analysis format described above the firm was represented choosing between alternative processes or activities. Each activity described the amount of each resource or intermediate good required to produce a unit of output. If we are producing grain, an activity would list the amount of land and fertilizer and other inputs necessary in order to produce one bushel of wheat. The farmer can choose from among large number of such activities and since each such process uses land and fertilizers in different proportions, the farmer is able to substitute land for fertilizer by substituting a process which uses a large amount of land relative to fertilizer for one which uses relatively less land. Should the price of land fall relative to fertilizer, a process using more land and less fertilizer is adopted to replace a process using relatively less land. In this way, the linear model achieves substitution in production. Similarly, it is possible to represent economies of scale in a linear model of the firm. Some processes may be feasible at high levels of output but not at low levels of output. If the firm can reduce unit costs by using the processes which are feasible at high output levels, it achieves economies of scale.

There is no reason in principle, why the multisectoral model should not make full use of the detailed information which (at least in theory) is available to each firm (including information about activities which are not actually used). From an empirical point of view however, this is an impossible task. Detailed specifications about each firm would rapidly take us beyond the capacity limits of any known computer. Furthermore, such detailed knowledge about individual firms is considered confidential. Only in rare instances, as in the case of regulated industries, is it possible to obtain data at the level of the establishment. When information about processes is available it is released at a level of aggregation which combines the activities of many firms. The firm data which is lost in the process of aggregation is the sacrifice which must be made in order to study the interdependence of the system as a whole.

This approach should be compared to partial equilibrium analysis where as noted above, data at the level of the firm are studied intensively under the assumption that each industry is independent of every other industry. It is precisely this partial equilibrium assumption which becomes the object of research in the multisectoral model. The results obtained, therefore, should be interpreted as indicating the direction of change at the level of the industry rather than at level of the firm. Although the magnitudes indicate the intensiveness of the underlying pressures for expansion or contraction in each industry, they do not reveal the actual amount that would be expected in free trade. The assumptions adopted in this study are those which are appropriate for inter-industry analysis. These assumptions must now be considered.

ECONOMIES OF SCALE

Under conditions of free trade the smaller nations of the world such as Canada have an increased opportunity to establish specialization in lines of production which are not presently open. In nations such as Norway or Sweden, the home market is too small for firms to fully exploit economies of scale. In the case of Canada, the U.S. market could provide an opportunity for Canadian firms to expand beyond the capacity of the home market if the U.S. tariff were eliminated. It is unrealistic to assume, however, that Canada can achieve this without reducing its own tariffs. For purposes of analysis it must be assumed that foreign nations will expect to have the same access to Canada that Canada expects to achieve abroad. Under these circumstances, it is by no means clear whether the industries benefitting from economies of scale will choose a location in Canada or somewhere else in the world.

Studies of economies of scale are of little help in this regard because they merely establish the fact that economies of scale are either present or absent in a particular industry. The technological advantages of scale are operative anywhere in the world. Without recourse to a multisectoral analysis, and locational studies it is not possible to predict which industries in Canada might expand and which cannot. Technological information on economies of scale is insufficient to determine the slope of the long-run industry supply curve unless we have additional information on the prices of resources and intermediate goods.

This point was established in the literature long ago by Robinson (1941). An industry which can realize economies of scale in a technological sense may have either a rising or a declining long-run cost curve. As noted above, an industry which expands attracts resources and intermediate goods away from all other industries and, in the process, bids up the costs of those intermediate goods and resources which it requires in greatest proportion. These rising costs may offset the technological effects of economies of scale. The relative prices of intermediate goods and resources determine comparative costs. Using the multisectoral model one can determine the relative prices and exchange rate which will clear the market for intermediate goods, resources, and foreign exchange. Ideally, one would incorporate economies of scale within the multisectoral model itself but, as noted above, it is an impossible task empirically to include detailed data at the firm level in a multisectoral model. Some type of compromise is needed.

The empirical research on economies of scale establishes technological relationships between inputs and outputs. These relationships are independent of the actual observed conditions of supply and demand in any nation and of relative prices. This information may therefore be used as an independent source of supplementary information. This is the approach adopted in this study.

As an illustration one might take the case of automobile manufacturing in Canada. Research on the subject indicates that technological economies of scale are present. The data used for the multisectoral model described in chapter two pre-date the Automobile Agreement of 1965 (which virtually established free trade between Canada and the US in automobiles and parts). Nevertheless, the model indicates that under constant returns to scale, the automobile industry would be expected to expand in free trade. The two bits of information together are mutually reinforcing and give us a strong case for predicting the actual expansion of production that was eventually observed after the Automobile Agreement. Cost and price changes favoured the automobile industry in Canada and since economies of scale were possible one would expect even greater expansion. Similarly, the multisectoral model should correctly predict contraction of a Canadian industry. US industries are already close to exhausting economies of scale and Canadian industries can, at best, reach the level of scale achieved in the US. In the industries where the simulation indicates contraction, the Canadian industry will face increased factor cost in free trade.[4]

In order to prevent errors due to the constant returns to scale assumption, output levels in each industry are constrained preventing contraction or expansion beyond a ten per cent limit. With this amount of slack, it should be possible to identify the principal industries in which expansion can be expected and to distinguish these from the industries which are expected to decline. To go beyond the ten per cent change would constitute an unwarranted extrapolation of the industry level results.

SUBSTITUTION IN PRODUCTION

When one aggregates to the level of industries, information at the firm level concerning the possibilities for substitution of one resource for another or one intermediate good for another is obviously lost. In the specification of the multisectoral model it is implicitly assumed, for example, that land and fertilizer are used in fixed proportions in the production of wheat. As noted above, when the prices of factors of production change, there are economic incentives for producers to substitute lower priced factors of production for higher priced factors. In multisectoral models such as the one employed in this book, it is assumed that substitutions in production do not occur when factor prices change and, therefore, implicitly there is a single process which can produce each commodity. The implications of this assumption are perhaps best appreciated if one contrasts the assumptions used in the multisectoral approach with the assumptions normally adopted in partial equilibrium models.

The first point to consider is the roll of intermediate products. In partial equilibrium models these are usually ignored entirely under the assumption that all firms are vertically integrated. When intermediate goods are integrated into partial equilibrium models, they are incorporated, as in the multisectoral model, under the assumption that there are no substitutions in production. The partial equilibrium model achieves greater flexibility, however, with regard to assumptions made concerning the roles of labour and capital. In partial equilibrium models, these two factors of production are almost always assumed to be substitutable one for the other while in the multisectoral model it is assumed that they are used in fixed proportion to output. In considering these results, the reader must decide whether or not this more rigid assumption in the multisectoral model may lead to deceptive conclusions.

It is the purpose of the multisectoral model adopted in this book to determine the direction of change in each industry under conditions simulating free trade. Theoretical studies show that the direction of change might be exactly the opposite of the direction indicated by the model if there are factor intensity reversals occurring.[5] Empirical evidence indicates, however, that over a wide range of factor price changes, factor intensity reversals are not likely to occur.[6] Nevertheless, the reader should keep in mind that the simulation proceeds under the assumption that there are no substitutions in production at all. Even though we correctly forecast the direction of change at the level of the industry, there may be some firms which, compared to others, have greater facility to adjust to changes in factor prices. By changing production methods these firms can succeed more than is predicted by the multi-sectoral model and hence may move against the tide predicted for the industry as a whole.

ASSUMPTIONS CONCERNING PRICES

The theory of effective tariffs is a substantial and growing literature. It is a frequently adopted assumption in this literature and, in fact, in the literature on tariffs generally that tariffs establish differentials between the foreign and home prices equal to the amount of the home tariff. In the theoretical literature it has been the general practice to assume, for purposes of exposition, that the tariffs in all but the home nation are zero. It follows, from profit maximizing assumptions, that the price of goods imported into the home nation will exceed the price in the nation of export by the amount of the home tariff. This point has also been exploited in empirical research in Canada and elsewhere.[7]

In a more general model this pricing rule must be extended to apply to goods exported from the home nation. If there are tariffs in the foreign nation, under profit maximizing assumptions, the price in the foreign nation will exceed the home price by the amount of the tariff in the foreign nation. Since exports of Canada are imports in the foreign nation, this logic merely extends to the case of foreign nations the same rule that is assumed to apply in the home nation. Even this extension is not entirely satisfactory, however, because many firms in both nations will not price up to the full amount of tariff protection available.

Until quite recently, there has been a minor omission in the literature of international economics in that there is no explicit statement of the pricing conditions necessary in a general model with many commodities, and although these conditions are part of the common knowledge[8] of international economics, it is not impossible that this omission has occasionally caused some confusion. The assumptions adopted in this book follow the exposition found in Kemp (1969, chap. 1) which may be stated as follows:

1. In the absence of price discrimination, the price in the home nation less the tariff in the home nation must be less than or equal to the price in the foreign nation. This follows whenever there is profit maximizing behaviour at the level of the firm (even if the firm is monopolistic). If, for example, the price in Canada less the Canadian tariff were higher than the US price, US producers could increase their profits by selling more in Canada and less in the US. Imports into Canada would rise causing the price in Canada to fall relative to the US price until the Canadian price less the Canadian tariff should equal the US price. This equality will hold for goods imported into Canada in sufficient quantity but it is not assumed to hold for all commodities. For many commodities the Canadian price will be determined by local conditions of supply and demand and the Canadian price less Canadian tariff will be less than the US price. Such producers will have more protection than they actually require to isolate themselves from foreign competitors.

2. This same pricing rule must also be applied to the foreign nation. The price in the foreign nation less the tariff in the foreign nation must be less than or equal to the price in Canada. If the foreign price less the foreign tariff is greater than the Canadian price, profit maximizing firms would initiate or expand exports increasing the Canadian price and reducing the foreign price until the foreign price less foreign tariff should equal the Canadian price. If there is a substantial flow of exports, the Canadian price will be equal to the foreign price less the foreign tariff, otherwise the inequality will hold.

3. When the inequality holds in both (1) and (2) above, prices in Canada vary according to local conditions of supply and demand.

As long as the tariff schedules at home and abroad do not change, there is a fixed rule that links the Canadian price to the price in the foreign market in all cases where the equality holds in (1) and (2). Since we assume that Canadian production of commodities (other than resources) is too small to affect world prices, this fixed rule is sufficient to determine Canadian prices of traded goods provided we know foreign prices, the Canadian tariff, and the foreign tariff. The fixed rule is, in fact, used as a device to set some initial values in the simulation in a manner described in chapter three.

It should be emphasized, however, that we do *not* assume that a fixed rule holds in all commodity groups nor is it assumed to hold in any particular group if the tariff at home or abroad should change. Whether or not the rule should apply will be determined as part of the outcome of the simulation and there will be many cases where the strict inequality will hold. The rules concerning prices follow from the assumptions (1) that firms are maximizing profits, and (2) that there is no price discrimination across international borders. Neither assumption excludes monopolistic pricing. In practice, behaviour consistent with the second assumption is enforced by public regulation and public attitudes. To sell abroad at a price less than costs in the home market is contrary to the rules of GATT which are enforced by national anti-dumping laws. Public opinion is easily rallied against international price discrimination. Therefore, the forces moving the system toward the assumed pricing conditions are economic, social, and legal.

OTHER ASSUMPTIONS

In order to simplify the analysis, it is assumed, in all phases of the numerical work in this study that United States prices can serve to represent world prices. This is justified by the large percentage of trade between Canada and the US and by the competitiveness and size of the US market. These factors establish a presumption that US prices are close to the minimum of world prices. But there is a further implicit assumption. All Canadian producers (except for those in the resource sector) are regarded as price takers. This implies that either (1) there is no single Canadian producer so large that he can set the world price, or (2) given such a producer exists, he is either unwilling or otherwise unable to use his market power to establish the price in the home and foreign market.

As noted above, the expression for aggregate demand in the simulation is based on the assumption that increments of aggregate consumer expenditure will follow the same proportions as total expenditure in the base year. This assumption was needed because time series data classified by commodity were not available. The actual results of the simulations indicate that the proportionality assumption must hold over a range of about five per cent of base year expenditure and it was concluded that, given the data limitations, over this range, a greater accuracy could not be achieved with an alternative representation of aggregate demand.

In his interpretation of the outcome of this research, the reader should also bear in mind that the model adopted incorporates the assumption that resource utilization rates are fixed. An error is introduced to the extent that changes in the Canadian and US tariffs may alter the amounts of resources supplied to the Canadian economy after the tariff reduction. For two reasons we judged that the error from this source would be small and that, in any case, it would not alter the direction of change observed in the simulation. First of all and most importantly, the tariffs which at present apply to resources are either zero or close to zero on most items, and we therefore expect that the price changes in the resource sector caused by the tariff removal will be small or zero. Secondly, it was decided at an early stage in this research that it would be more realistic to assume that the quantitative restrictions at present protecting agricultural resources would also be in effect after tariffs and other trade restrictions are eliminated. These quantitative restrictions are forces stabilizing resource flows internationally.[9]

Transportation and shipping enter into the model as a separate industry supplying services to other industries. Transport costs, therefore reflect the actual cost per dollar of output in the observed 1961 period. If the tariff should change the average distance that goods are carried in an industry, it would change the value of this coefficient and bias the outcome of the simulation. It is assumed implicitly that the cost of transportation between two points within Canada can be compared to the cost between a point in Canada and a point in the US. The results of this study are strictly correct only with regard to those points of destination in Canada where the cost of shipping from a Canadian plant is the same as from a comparable US plant. We may assume that the number of such points are quite numerous because of the extensive East-West border between Canada and the US and because the population of Canada is concentrated near the US border.

AGGREGATION AND DATA ORGANIZATION

Aggregation is an unfortunate yet necessary step in any research which attempts to study the economy beyond the level of the firm. Typically, models of this type are based on a level of aggregation which produces from 14 to 30 sectors. The accuracy of a multisectoral model is greater the greater the number of sectors considered because, with a larger number of categories, there are fewer cases in which dissimilar goods are classified together. The data in this study were passed through preliminary screening prior to the final aggregation and, because of the large number of classes, the effects of misclassification could be reduced to a minimum.

The basic statistical source for this project is a set of input-output tables which were organized at Statistics Canada according to a 189-level industrial and 644-level commodity classification. This information is ultimately brought down (in a manner described in chapter three) to a 103-level of classification. Prior to this aggregation each commodity was studied at the 644-level to determine whether in 1961 and 1964 it played the role of (1) a resource commodity; (2) a non-competing import; (3) an import competing commodity; (4) a domestic commodity; or (5) an exportable commodity. Resource commodities, according to our definition, are the first measurable product of land. Live animals and copper ore are examples of resource commodities. Non-competing imports are commodities, such as coffee, which are not produced in Canada at all. Import competing commodities are those which are both produced in Canada and imported in Canada. Domestic commodities are produced in Canada but are neither imported nor exported. Exportable goods are those which are produced in Canada and also exported from Canada.

Goods at the 644-level were aggregated in such a way that each of the commodities included in one of the groups at the 103-level carries the same designation as every other. Domestic goods were aggregated with only domestic goods and goods which were exported were aggregated only with other goods which were exported, etc. Therefore, all of the commodities at the 103-level of classification are also identified with one of the five categories described above.

The aggregation into industries follows the principle that goods should be classified together if they are physically similar and if they have similar responses to assumed changes in economic circumstances.[10] Non-competing imports, for example, consist of such items as raw rubber, cotton and coffee. It is not rash to assume that these will never be produced in Canada and clearly it would be an error to classify these with commodities which are typically exported. Exports are vulnerable and sensitive to changes in foreign tariffs. A rise in the US tariff would affect Canadian production through the Canadian export sector. Import competing goods are responsive to changes in the Canadian tariff and affect Canadian production through the Canadian industries competing with imports. In describing the steel sector, for example, it is necessary to distinguish between that part of it which exported in 1961, that part which was import competing in 1961 and that part which was domestic in 1961. These three industrial classifications will respond differently to free trade or to any other hypothetical situation. Export industries tend to increase in free trade and the output of the import competing industries tends to fall. Since different economic forces operate in these different categories, production will move in different directions and, therefore, they should not be aggregated together.

In the initial conditions of the model (before any simulation experiments) the pricing rules described in the previous section were used to establish initial values for the model in some industries. If a commodity was imported in 1961, it was assumed that the Canadian price less the Canadian tariff was equal to the US price. This rule was assumed to be operative in twenty-six industries. If a commodity was exported in 1961, it was assumed that the Canadian price was equal to the US price less the US tariff. This rule was assumed to be operative in nine industries. Aside from these initializing assumptions, no strict rule is assumed to hold in any industry. In the simulation all prices are free to vary within the range permitted by the Canadian and foreign tariff.

COMPARATIVE ADVANTAGE

In the standard model of trade comparative advantage is revealed by (1) a comparison of relative costs between two nations when each is operating under conditions of autarky, or (2) by a comparison of production levels under idealized conditions of free trade in which all price distorting taxes are absent. The former method is obviously beyond reach empirically. The second, however, can be achieved within the scope of the multisectoral model. We therefore adopt a special definition of free trade in this analysis. In the situation described as free trade it is assumed that all taxes and subsidies which are specific to particular industries are zero. With this assumption one is able to produce a simulation which is as close as possible to the ideal required by the second approach. The simulation indicates the direction of change needed in each industry if the system is to move toward its comparative advantage.

The operation of this method can be illustrated using the case of a small nation producing two commodities using two resources. Under idealized conditions such a nation will specialize in the production of the commodity which uses relatively more of its abundant resource and this commodity will be exported. A tariff on imports will, to some extent, retard this development by encouraging expansion of the import competing commodity. Resources and labour, which otherwise would be used to produce the exported commodity, will be bid over to the production of the import competing good. A simulation of this simple case would reveal the direction of change in the output of each industry as we shift from the tariff situation to comparative advantage under free trade. It would indicate that the level of production in the export industry is higher in free trade and that production in the import competing industry is lower.

The multisector model works in a similar manner except that the outcome of the simulation will no longer be so obvious. In general, we expect that the export sector will expand in free trade but it does not follow that production will expand in every export class. Exports of some commodities may have expanded beyond the optimal level and will decline under free trade. Even if export demand does rise as expected in a given industry, it does not follow that total demand for the output of that industry has increased. Production in any particular industry is, at least in part, shipped as an intermediate product to other industries and this demand may have declined enough to offset the growth of exports. In such a case, production may decline because of the decrease in the demand for intermediate goods. Similarly, in the import competing sector we expect a general decline in production and an increase in imports but there will be exceptions in individual industries. Some will need to expand in order to produce more intermediate goods for other industries which have expanded. In some industries, imports will not increase and may decline to zero. In the many domestic industries, the pattern of change is even less obvious.

All industries will compete with each other for limited supplies of resources and labour. With the introduction of free trade there are changes in relative prices and the exchange rate and some industries which were not competitive with foreign production under the tariff may become competitive after the general change in relative prices. The results of all of these factors act simultaneously in the simulation to determine the output levels that would prevail in free trade. Operating in a manner similar to the market process, the simulation selects production, import and export activities in such a manner as to supply a maximum of consumer goods without exceeding resource supplies and without using more foreign exchange than is available.

The difference in the level of output in the tariff situation as compared to free trade indicates the direction required if the economy is to move toward its comparative advantage. As we indicated above, however, it is important to keep in mind that each industry is, in fact, an aggregation of many individual firms and enterprises. The actual change in any particular firm may be different from the industry as a whole. The sectoral analysis is a device which permits one to study the general equilibrium aspects of tariff adjustment but the results are not sufficient to determine the outcome in the case of an individual firm. The individual firm may be idiosyncratic in its resource requirements or may be able to realize economies of scale and hence may expand while the industry as a whole is declining. Some firms may switch from an import competing role to exporting. These possibilities demonstrate the importance of supplementary research along partial equilibrium lines. At our present level of aggregation we do not expect to discover cases of trade switching in individual firms and it is assumed that major changes of this type will not occur at the sectoral level.

Comparative advantage is revealed by the outcome of the simulation in which all Canadian and US tariffs are set at zero and in which all production taxes and subsidies are set at zero. If production taxes and subsidies are not set at zero, the simulation will be to that extent distorted and fail to reflect comparative advantage. For expositional convenience the simulation with all taxes and tariffs set at zero is hereafter called the free trade simulation.

COMPARISON TO PARTIAL EQUILIBRIUM

The data for this study were organized with the simulation primarily in mind. Nevertheless, they may be readily adopted for certain types of partial equilibrium interpretations. Such supplemental analysis may be used (1) to help understand or explain the functioning of the multisectoral model; (2) to check the intuitive reasonableness of the results; and (3) as an aid to establish a tariff strategy. A number of partial equilibrium measures are computed which can supplement the multisectoral analysis.

WEIGHTED AVERAGE CANADIAN AND US TARIFFS

By virtue of the Canadian tariff a producer located in Canada can compete on equal terms with foreign producers with lower costs provided the foreign producer's costs are no lower per unit of output than the amount of Canadian specific duty payable. If Canadian costs rise above this, economic forces exist which encourage further penetration of the Canadian market. The Canadian tariff is a partial equilibrium index of the protection of the Canadian market against foreign competition measuring the maximum amount that Canadian costs can rise above US costs per unit of output. The partial equilibrium index for an industrial classification as a whole is equal to a weighted average of the Canadian tariff with Canadian industrial outputs of individual commodities serving as weights. Similarly, the US tariff is a partial equilibrium measure of protection of the US market. A weighted average of the US tariff using Canadian output levels as weights is a partial equilibrium index measuring the amount that the US market is protected against Canadian competition.

Weighted average tariffs are computed for both the US and Canada for the year 1961 and for Canada alone in the post-Kennedy period. These data are presented for all industrial groups in Table 3.3 and are also shown in the summary tables of the remaining chapters. While these weighted average tariffs are logically correct in the analytical context for which they are employed, great caution must be urged if they are used to compare the general level of tariffs in the US to those of Canada. If such a comparison is logically possible at all, it would somehow need to take both the US and Canadian weights into account. The average tariffs defined in this study are partial equilibrium measures used to compare the level of protection in one Canadian industry to that of another.

The weighted average tariff computed for each industry measures the amount of direct tariff protection available in each classification. In general this amount of protection will be of greater importance the greater the flow over the Canadian tariff of imports competing with local production. To the extent that there was a large flow of imports in 1961 over a high Canadian tariff there is greater probability that the multisectoral analysis will predict a decline in production under free trade.

Similarly, the weighted average US tariff is a partial equilibrium indicator of the amount that a Canadian industry is blocked from the US market. If Canadian firms producing exports are to receive the same unit revenue in the US market as they received in the Canadian market, they must charge a price greater than the

Canadian price by the amount of the US tariff. A weighted average of the US tariff (taking Canadian outputs as weights) indicates the amount that the Canadian producing sector must increase its price in the US market if it is to sell in the US market with the same return as in Canada. The US tariff is most important to Canadian export industries and, therefore, in industries where the weighted average US tariff is large and where there is a large flow of Canadian goods over the US tariff the probabilities are greater that the simulation will indicate an expansion.

These guidelines are helpful but one must keep in mind that they can do no more than reflect the data at a point in time. The Canadian tariff may be so high that it blocks imports entirely or the US tariff may be prohibitive with regard to certain Canadian production that would otherwise be exported.

INDIRECT EFFECTS OF TARIFFS

The Canadian or US tariff on a particular commodity not only affects the price of that commodity in Canada as compared to the price in the US, it also affects the costs of all goods produced in both nations. Because of the tariff, Canadian producers find that the cost of intermediate goods purchased from the import-competing sector are raised by, perhaps, the full amount of the Canadian tariff. We refer to this extra cost as antiprotection. High levels of antiprotection may prevent an industry from reaching the level required by comparative advantage. When Canadian producers make purchases of intermediate goods from the export sector, on the other hand, they find that this anti-protection is somewhat offset. In the export sector the price of goods in Canada tend to be cheaper by the amount of the US tariff. This is an indirect source of protection and may induce some industries to expand beyond the relative size required by comparative advantage. The sum of these two effects on intermediate goods prices we call the 'cost effect per dollar of output' and this is shown in columns 6 and 7 of the second summary table in chapters four through nine. It is also displayed for all industries in Table 3.3. We usually refer to the cost effect per dollar of output as the amount of antiprotection because with one exception it operates to increase the cost of intermediate goods. No one familiar with the Canadian situation will be surprised by this fact. The antiprotection of the Canadian tariff predominates over the indirect protection of the US tariff because exports to the US are mostly resource goods or goods in the early phases of processing, and the US tariff tends to be low or zero on these goods, and hence the FOB cost of such goods to Canadians is no lower than the cost to Americans.

The estimate of the indirect effects of the Canadian and US tariff are derived from data organized in a way that is particularly suitable for making such calculations. As noted above, the distinction has been carefully maintained throughout between exportable, importable and domestic goods through all phases of data organization. The indirect effects are based on the 103-level table which, compared to other studies of this type, is a rather low level of aggregation and, therefore, it was possible to obtain partial equilibrium estimates of indirect effects for a comparatively large number of industrial classifications. No sector or industry is omitted from the calculations. Indirect effects of the tariff are obtained for mining and agriculture as well as for manufacturing. The indirect cost effects reveal the impact of both the Canadian and US tariff (not just the Canadian tariff) as they affect costs in all industries. These effects should be subtracted from the direct protection of the Canadian tariff to obtain the amount of net protection. One would anticipate that, in the free trade simulation, the industries having the greatest amount of net protection in this partial equilibrium sense would, in general, constitute the group most likely to decline.

One might, alternatively, anticipate the outcome of the simulation along a slightly different line. Prices in the import competing sector are generally higher relative to prices in the export sector. Industries which use a large proportion of their costs to purchase intermediate products from the import competing sector are at a disadvantage. Under free trade industries making large purchases of goods from the import competing sector should find that their costs have fallen relatively and one would expect that they would expand. Similarly, industries which purchase intermediate goods from the export sector will discover that relative prices will tend to be higher in free trade. The percentage of costs spent to purchase goods from the import competing sector, export sector, and the resource sector are computed for each industry and displayed in the various tables of part two of this study. These various partial equilibrium indicators are related to the outcome of the simulation in the analysis below.

NON-TARIFF BARRIERS

Nothing has been said so far concerning non-tariff barriers. Since, in determining comparative advantage, it is desired that the model should reflect free trade conditions as closely as possible, no constraints are introduced to take these into account. Nevertheless, it is obvious that non-tariff barriers establish an amount of protection which is not reflected in the weighted average tariffs computed for each industry. Compared to other nations in the world, Canada is relatively free of non-tariff barriers and consequently there are fewer cases where these come into consideration. When it is possible to identify a non-tariff barrier with a particular industrial classification, there will be some attention given to it in the sectoral summaries of part two of this book. However, most non-tariff barriers are too general to be dovetailed into the classification framework and we therefore give a very brief summary here of the most important Canadian non-tariff barriers.[11]

1. Industrial subsidies are considered a form of non-tariff barrier when they apply in the import competing sector. In the multisectoral model such subsidies are netted out against the amount of commodity tax paid in each industry. In the free trade simulation all commodity taxes and subsidies are set at zero.

2. Importation of certain items listed in Schedule C of the Canadian Tariff Schedule are prohibited. Prohibition of used automobiles, used airplanes and oleomargarine are clearly intended as protective devices.

3. Any item found on the Import Control List is subject to import licensing under the Export and Import Permits Act. Coffee, sugar, and dairy products appear on this list and recently cotton yarn and men's and boy's clothing have been added.

4. All governments, including Canada, purchase higher-priced home production in preference to lower-cost foreign supplies.

5. Similarly, most countries of the world prohibit imports of goods which fail to meet the industrial, health, or safety standards of the home nation. Foreign producers, in these cases, must set-up special production runs in order to produce for the Canadian market. The extra cost involved may be considered a non-tariff barrier.

6. Canada and the US are among the few major trading nations in the world which have not adopted the Brussels Tariff Nomenclature. Foreign nations claim that the uncertainty concerning import classification in Canada is another form of non-tariff barrier.

7. Under certain conditions the Canadian valuation for duty is 'constructed.' Foreign nations allege that this is also a source of uncertainty and that it is occasionally used in a way that is discriminatory.

8. In Canada retail sales of liquor, beer, and wine are either licensed to private vendors or sold directly by provincial central authorities. In either case retail sales are operated so as to give local producers a substantial sales advantage over foreign producers.

9. Since the early sixties a system has gradually emerged in which the higher density-low wage nations of the world have been persuaded to impose quotas on their exports of certain items. These 'voluntary export restraints' usually apply to exports of textiles. In Canada they have been applied also to imports from Japan of stainless steel flatware, plywood and radio or television receiving tubes. Importation of men's and boy's gloves from China has also been subject to voluntary export restraints.

DESCRIPTIVE MATERIAL

The free trade simulation determines the output levels which result in optimal resource use. Industries at the early stages of processing tend to be identified with a single resource while those at the end stages of processing are usually identified with several resources or, in some cases, cannot be identified precisely with any resource at all. In some industries, as in the case of metal products, the resource identity of each industry is obvious. In other sectors, such as chemicals, the resource identity of the various industries is not so obvious.

In their public statements Canadians have indicated a preference for greater resource processing in Canada and for industries in the later stages of processing over industries at the earlier stages. The relationship between resource use, trade and the degree of processing is one which interests Canadians because it has direct policy implications and because it explains, in part, why output in certain industries is relatively large compared to production in the United States. Readers interested in such policy questions can make use of the descriptive tables in the later chapters of this book. Value added and the percentage of total output shipped as intermediate goods are displayed for each industry. In order to examine the flow of intermediate products between related industries, special tables of commodity flows are prepared for selected sectors. These are displayed in the tables of part two with data on tariffs and trade. All of this material is presented on a common definitional basis.

DISCRIMINANT ANALYSIS

Discriminant analysis may be used to establish the relationship between the free trade simulation and the descriptive tariff, tax, and trade data discussed above. The simulation results are used to define two groups. The first group (group I) consists of the sixteen industries which expanded the most in the simulation, and the second (group II) consists of the sixteen which contracted the most. Each group is characterized by the eleven variables defined in Table 1.1. Using the data for group I and group II, the discriminant analysis determines a set of weights or coefficients for the variables. The coefficients form a linear combination of the variables, which is an index used to classify each industry. If the index for industry i is greater than an amount determined by the discriminant analysis, it will be classified in group I; if less than this amount it is classified in group II. If the sign of the coefficient for a particular variable is positive, it means that the larger the value of the variable, the greater the likelihood, *ceteris paribus*, that the industry considered will expand in free trade. If the coefficient carries a negative sign and is numerically large, the industry will, *ceteris paribus*, more likely be among those which contract in free trade.

TABLE 1.1

Estimated weights for four discriminant functions

	Coefficients for discriminant function			
Variable	(1)	(2)	(3)	(4)
1 US tariff	5.50	3.85	4.20	3.67
2 Canadian tariff	−14.52	omitted	omitted	omitted
3 Anti-protection	24.00	omitted	omitted	omitted
4 Net protection	omitted	−13.77	−14.03	−13.19
5 Percentage of costs spent in the export sector	0.45	0.46	0.46	0.43
6 Percentage of costs spent in the import competing sector	0.11	0.06	0.06	0.07
7 Resource content	−0.13	−0.12	−0.12	omitted
8 Intermediate shipments	−0.06	−0.06	−0.06	−0.06
9 Commodity taxes	0.20	0.47	0.46	0.65
10 Exports per dollar	5.50	5.26	5.12	2.19
11 Imports per dollar of output	0.23	0.30	omitted	omitted
Application of Chi-square test				
Proportion of correct classifications based on 16 most expanded and 16 most contracted industries	$\frac{24}{32}$	$\frac{25}{32}$	$\frac{25}{32}$	$\frac{28}{32}$
Value of χ^2	8.0	10.1	10.1	18.0

The technique can be illustrated with a hypothetical case in which we have but two variables. Let s_{1i} be the Canadian tariff and s_{2i} be the US tariff for industry i; then the discriminant analysis will determine a β_1 and β_2 which can be used to form the discriminant function

$$I_i = \beta_1 s_{1i} + \beta_2 s_{2i},$$

where I_i is the classifying index. The discriminant analysis also determines a value I_0. If $I_0 < I_i$, industry i should be classified with group I. The sign of the coefficient β_1 indicates whether s_{1i} is characteristic of group I or group II. If, for example, $\beta_1 > 0$ it means that industries confronted by high US tariffs will more likely have a high index I_i and, since I_i will then be greater than I_0, industry i will be classified with the expanding industries. If the 32 industries are classified by the discriminant function, they will display a maximum variance between categories relative to the pooled variance within categories.[12] The two groups will then differ by an amount which is maximum in this sense.

The test based on the χ^2 distribution can be used to determine the success of the estimated discrimination function in distinguishing between contracting and expanding industries. To illustrate the interpretation we refer below to the co-classification is known in advance, one can determine the number of classifications correctly determined by the discriminant function. Under the hypothesis that the number of successful classifications took place at random, a value of χ^2 is determined which can be used in a manner illustrated below to test the significance of the classification obtained from the discriminant function (Press 1973, 382).

Results of the discrimination analysis are displayed in Table 1.1. The variables discussed in the sections above appear on the left-hand side in this table. The columns of Table 1.1 represent coefficients for four different discriminant functions. These coefficients identify the variables with either the contracting or expanding industries. To illustrate the interpretation we refer below to the coefficients in column 1 only.

The reader will note that the weight in row 1 which is applied to the US tariff is positive indicating that industries facing a high US tariff tend, *ceteris paribus,* to be classified among those which expand in free trade. Similarly, item two in column 1 is negative indicating that industries protected by high Canadian tariffs are, *ceteris paribus,* more likely to be classified with those which contract in free trade. Inspection of the remainder of column 1 can establish other characteristics which tend to bring industries into one classification or the other. According to these coefficients, industries classified with those which expand (1) face high U.S. tariffs; (2) are given little or no shelter from the Canadian tariff; (3) face high levels of antiprotection; (4) use a large percentage of costs to make purchases from the export sector; (5) use a relatively large percentage of cost to purchase from the import competing sector; (6) use a lesser percentage of costs to purchase resources; (7) ship fewer intermediate goods to other industries (and hence produce more end products); (8) pay more in commodity taxes; (9) export a larger percentage of output; (10) import a larger percentage of output.

The economic interpretation of this outcome is discussed below where we shall also call attention to some of the features of columns 2, 3, and 4. To judge the statistical significance of the result, the reader should refer to the last two unnumbered lines in Table 1.1. The success of the weights in Table 1.1 in classifying industries was tested by applying the weights to the thirty two industries of groups I and II. The second to last line in the table indicates the proportion of correct classifications. The discriminant function with the weights shown in column 1 of Table 1.1, for example, gives a success rate of 24 out of 32 cases.

To test the hypothesis that these successes took place at random versus the hypothesis that the discrimination procedure did better than just chance, we calculate the value of χ^2 (with one degree of freedom) shown on the last line of Table 1.1. Since a value of χ^2 this large or larger has a probability of less than 0.005, we reject the hypothesis that the results are random.

A large number of formulations (motivated by the theoretical considerations described above) were tried using different combinations of these variables. Columns 1, 2, 3 and 4 are representative of the results. In the discriminant function with the coefficients shown in column 1, all variables are included giving 24 correct classifications. A higher ratio of correct classifications can be obtained, however, by combining direct protection (line 2) and antiprotection (line 3) into a single variable, net protection (line 4) as in column 2. From column 3 it is determined that the success to failure ratio is maintained if variable 11, imports per dollar of output is left out of the discriminant function. Column 4 is the discriminant function with the highest number of correct classifications. This function has the same variables as column 3 except for the fact that variable 7, resource content, is omitted.

The coefficients on each line of Table 1.1 are consistent in sign and magnitude. Because of this, the interpretation of the role of any particular variable is the same regardless of which function is examined. The discriminant function, therefore, may be regarded as accurately describing the general characteristics of the adjustment process in the simulation. One's confidence in the results is enhanced if the general characteristics of the simulation are in agreement with the partial and general equilibrium theory of tariffs.

ECONOMIC INTERPRETATION OF THE DISCRIMINANT ANALYSIS

From the theory of tariffs and, indeed from intuition alone one expects, first of all that the industries which expand in the free trade would *ceteris paribus* be those facing a higher US tariff. The coefficients on line 1 of Table 1.1 are all positive as required. A second result suggested by theory is contraction in free trade in the classifications where *ceteris paribus* protection from the Canadian tariff is greatest. The negative coefficient on line 2 is in agreement with this expectation. As a third theoretical expectation it would be anticipated that *ceteris paribus* a firm is more likely to expand in free trade if, under the tariff, there is a high level of antiprotection. The coefficient on line 3 of Table 1.1 is fact positive, which again demonstrates agreement between the outcome in the simulation and theoretical expectations. As noted above, net protection can be used as a single variable to replace the Canadian tariff less antiprotection and this outcome (the negative coefficient on line 4 of Table 1.1) also agrees with theory.

To continue the comparison we consider the consequences in free trade of a decline in relative prices in the import competing sector which theory leads us to anticipate. As a consequence of lower prices, a firm located in the import competing sector would tend to decline relatively in free trade while firms having relatively large expenditures in the import competing sector would tend to expand because they would find that intermediate goods could be purchased at lower cost. Agreement between the outcome of the simulation and theory is confirmed in the case of the positive coefficients on line 6 but contradicted by the positive coefficient on line 11 which indicates expansion is likely in cases where there is a high ratio of imports per dollar of output. It will be noted, however, from columns 3 and 4, that imports per dollar of output can best be left out of the discriminant function (see line 11). As we point out again in the summary section of part two of this book, the Canadian tariff has a mixed effect in the import competing sector providing much less protection to the sector as a whole than in generally assumed.

The positive coefficients on line 10 of Table 1.1 are also in agreement with theory. The elimination of the US tariff in free trade should increase demand in the United States for Canadian output and increase the price and output in Canada of goods produced in the export sector. A rise in the Canadian price of intermediate goods in the export sector however should make contraction more probable in firms which use a large percentage of costs to purchase intermediate goods from the export sector. From Table 1.1 we see that the signs of the coefficients on line 5 are contrary to expectation. This paradox can be explained by two characteristics peculiar to the Canadian economy: (1) by the fact that the Canadian export sector is concentrated at the early stages of processing, and (2) by the fact that the United States tariff is low or zero in such cases. There is a general trend, discussed below, for firms at the end stage of processing to expand. These firms are the largest purchasers from the export sector because production in the export sector consists of a high proportion of intermediate goods. However since the United States tariffs on products at the early stages of processing are very low to start with, their elimination has very little practical effect on prices in the export sector and, therefore, contrary to expectation, the rise in relative prices in Canada under free trade is not so great as to prevent firms with large purchases from the export sector from expanding.

The tendency, in the simulation, for firms at the earlier stages of processing to contract is confirmed by line 8 of Table 1.1. The negative coefficients indicate that *ceteris paribus* a classification will be more likely to contract if the ratio of intermediate output to total output is high. Further corroboration is found on line 7 which indicates that contraction is more likely in a classification where resource content is large. The shift in the direction of end product production is again confirmed in part two of this book where the results are studied on a sector by sector basis.

THE COST OF THE TARIFF

In the classical argument for free trade, the gains from trade derive from international specialization and exchange. The tariffs in the home nation and in the foreign nation cause a divergence between internal relative costs and relative prices abroad. Gains from trade can be achieved in a small nation if production is reduced in lines where relative costs are greatest and increased in lines where relative costs are least. The balance in consumption is then maintained through international trade. The cost of the tariff is defined as the value of goods which must be extracted in the free trade situation in order to maintain the nation at the level of utility it achieved under protection (Johnson, 1960, 327-44). In order to estimate the cost of the tariff in the multisectoral model, the US and Canadian tariffs and all industry specific tariffs are set at zero to determine the maximum level of consumption possible in free trade. The cost of the tariff is the difference between this magnitude and the level of consumption under the tariff.

Simulation experiments used to measure the cost of the tariff were conducted in connection with two commodity bundles. In one set of experiments, household consumption in the 1961 proportions was used to measure the cost of the tariff. The programme in this case measured the increased amount of consumption technically possible from the 1961 resource base assuming all other final demand items constant. In the second set of experiments investment goods were used to measure the cost of the tariff. In these experiments, consumption and other final demand items are held constant and 1961 relative purchases of investment goods were used to specify the bundle of goods. In both cases the amount of increased output was calculated under the assumption that (1) the Canadian tariff is unilaterally eliminated, (2) that the US tariff is unilaterally eliminated, and (3) under the assumption that both the Canadian and US tariff are eliminated.

The cost of the tariff measured under various assumptions is indicated in Table 1.2. Under free trade it would be technically possible to obtain four per cent more consumer goods. A unilateral elimination of the Canadian or US tariff yields only a modest gain. Elimination of the Canadian tariff itself would make it technically possible to increase consumer goods by only 1.4 per cent and a unilateral elimination of the U.S. tariff would yield an increase of only two per cent to Canadians. The four per cent gain when both the Canadian and US tariffs are reduced is greater than the sum of both individually.

TABLE 1.2

Cost of the Canadian and US tariff

Tariff schedule set at level zero	Consumption cost		Investment cost	
	Dollars ($000)	Per cent	Dollars ($000)	Per cent
1 Canadian tariffs	342,995	1.36	770,344	5.33
2 United States tariffs	511,701	2.03	981,330	6.79
3 Tariffs in both nations	1,002,330	3.97	1,318,727	9.12

The cost of the tariff is considerably larger when measured in terms of investment goods. A unilateral reduction in the Canadian tariff would make it technically possible to obtain five per cent more investment goods than actually produced in 1961. The US tariff unilaterally reduced makes it possible to have seven per cent more investment goods from the resources used in 1961. If both tariffs were eliminated, it would be technically possible to produce nine per cent more investment goods. The tariff has a more inhibiting effect on economic growth than it has on the annual level of consumption. The cost of the tariff measured in terms of investment goods is larger in both percentage and absolute terms.

COST OF THE TARIFF: INTERPRETATION

The multisectoral model determines the maximum amount of the composite commodity that it is technically possible to obtain using the observed 1961 production techniques, the 1961 resource supplies, and the 1961 opportunity to trade as represented by US relative prices. The revenue effects of the tariff are explicitly built into the estimation method. In free trade the price of Canadian exports in the US is increased by the amount that US tariffs are reduced. Since by assumption, Canadian producers are price takers, Canadian exporters receive the higher US price and thereby earn more foreign exchange for Canada. A reduction of the Canadian tariff represents no loss of foreign exchange however because the foreign exchange cost of imports is exclusive of the Canadian tariff (which is paid with Canadian dollars). The Government of Canada will lose taxes equal to the amount of the lost tariff revenue but, as we show mathematically in chapter two, in free trade these revenues can be recovered by a general sales tax without affecting the optimal solution of the model. It is therefore technically possible to obtain the free trade solution with government expenditures and total tax collections unchanged. There are, however, a number of aspects of the estimation method that lead to an underestimate of the gain from trade.

One source of additional gain derives from substitution in consumption. The algorithm measures the increased amount of 1961 consumption available under free trade but consumers will be able to reach levels of satisfaction higher than the amount indicated. The change in relative prices under free trade will leave open an opportunity for consumers to substitute goods lower in price for commodities which are higher priced under free trade. A second source of additional gain derives from substitution in production. The increased output under free trade represents the amount that each firm can achieve without taking advantage of alternative production processes which are less costly per unit of output at world relative prices. Finally, there is an underestimate that results from the aggregation process. In the multisectoral simulation each producer in each classification is assumed to produce goods in the 1961 proportions regardless of the changes in the level of output for the classification as a whole. This is an implicit constraint on the algorithm which is not present in the actual situation. The errors which arise from these three sources are of unknown magnitude but not of unknown sign. All souces of error lead to an underestimation of the actual gain. Therefore, the increased production possible from international specialization and exchange will be at least as large as the amount measured in the multisectoral model.

A more serious error in the measured cost of the tariff arises from a different source. Modern writers and particularly Canadian economists would emphasize the gains arising from increased market size due to greater competitiveness within industries and to economies of scale. The discriminant analysis and the detailed descriptive material of part two indicate that, under free trade, there would be a shift toward end product production in Canada in the manufacturing sector (or at least there would be no decline). Furthermore, as the reader may verify from Table 1.3 there is very little change in the relative size of each sector. If so, there will likely be a movement in the direction of increased specialization within each sector in free trade rather than a shift in the size of one sector relative to another. Under such circumstances the magnitude of gain from economies of scale will become correspondingly more important.

In the tariff literature the gains from trade due to economies of scale are treated separately from the gains which arise in connection with international specialization and exchange. The figures in Table 1.2 represent estimates derived under the assumption that none of the expanding Canadian industries will realize economies of scale under free trade. In practice there may be substantial economies achieved through rationalization within each industrial sector with both Canada and the US specializing in particular product lines. Eastman and Stykolt (1967) provide documentary evidence that increased efficiency of this type is possible in many industries and Wonnacott and Wonnacott (1967) have shown additionally that locational factors would not be unfavourable in Canada

TABLE 1.3

Percentage change in output in six sectors

Sector	Percentage change
1 Iron and steel	+1.46
2 Nonferrous metal, electrical, and other producers	+2.40
3 Wood and paper products	+1.42
4 Chemical and chemical related industries	−2.87
5 Textile products	−6.47
6 Agriculture and food	−0.28

for specialization of this type. Wonnacott and Wonnacott (1967, 298) also provide an estimate of the gains from trade which include the gains obtained from economies of scale and increased competition. The authors arrive at an estimation of 6 per cent for the gains in factor incomes in free trade. To this they add 4.5 per cent of gross national expenditure as the gain from consumers' surplus due to lower prices and higher income. This results in an estimated cost of the tariff equal to 10.5 per cent. The cost estimated by the simulation comparable to this (shown in line three of Table 1.2) is 4 per cent of consumption or 2.6 per cent of gross national expenditure. This indicates that the gains from trade due to economies of scale and other sources of underestimation would be 7.9 per cent as a rough approximation. This implies that the gains through increased competitiveness and economies of scale are likely to be a greater source of gain through free trade than those realized through the classical mechanism of specialization and exchange. If the 7.9 per cent gain due to economies of scale, is expressed in terms of consumption it would amount to 12.1 per cent.

From these considerations it becomes clear that the percentages in Table 1.2 must be regarded as exceptionally conservative and therefore as representing a reliable lower bound estimate of the cost of the tariff. It should be emphasized that these figures are based on economic processes which were actually in use in 1961 and that it is demonstrated automatically in the estimation process that the output levels required to achieve the estimated gains from free trade are producible from the Canadian resource base and that the imports needed will satisfy the 1961 balance of trade constraint.

Because of the great difficulties in estimating the cost of the tariff, it is desirable that the task should be approached under various assumptions and using more than one method. For this reason it would not be appropriate to close this chapter without some discussion of Young's (1957) estimate of the cost of the tariff. This estimate should be interpreted as measuring the loss of income which is due to the effect of the Canadian tariff with the US remaining at its present level.

Professor Young (1957, 74) points out that his estimate of the cash cost of the tariff 'is an accounting magnitude rather than an economic one.' Nevertheless, Johnson (1960) has shown that his estimate can be given an economic interpretation. The results of his analysis imply that Young's (1957, 335) estimate leads to over-estimate of the cost of protection by the amount of economic rent earned in the domestic production of import substitutes and understates it by the amount of the consumption cost. Consequently, it is impossible to determine whether, as an economic magnitude, the Young estimate is too high or too low. Nevertheless, one can begin to obtain a general picture from the three methodologically different approaches. The Wonnacott estimate indicates that, with all considered, the US tariff, the Canadian tariff, and allowing for economies of scale, the cost of the tariff is about ten per cent. More than one-half of this would appear to be attributable to economies of scale and less than one-half to misallocations due to the Canadian and US tariff. The cost of the tariff is considerably larger when measured in terms of investment opportunities than when measured in terms of consumption opportunities.

CONCLUSIONS

The mathematical simulation described verbally in this chapter is an analytical technique which can be used to estimate the impact of the Canadian-United States tariff on the levels of output in Canadian industries. The actual levels of output under the tariff are compared to the levels of output predicted from the mathematical model when all tariffs are eliminated. This technique has the advantage that all relevant tariff and trade data are simultaneously utilized along with resource constraints to determine the predicted outcome and one is therefore likely to obtain results that are more accurate than could be obtained from an examination of tariffs or 'effective tariffs' by themselves.

On the basis of our results it is concluded that the Canadian-United States tariff schedules shifted Canada away from manufacturing and toward the earlier stages of processing. The tariff has failed to increase the output of end products in Canada above the level that would be expected in free trade. Industries that were classified with those expanding in free trade were *ceteris paribus*, those which produced the fewest intermediate products and which made relatively the smallest purchases of resources in dollar terms.

One's confidence in the mathematical model is greatly enhanced because of the close agreement between the adjustment processes observed in the simulation and those expected on the basis of theory and intuition. It was determined that the pattern of change to free trade could be very well characterized by the coefficients of the discriminant function displayed in Table 1.1. Firms which expand in free trade are those which face high United States tariffs and belong to producer classifications with low levels of net protection. This is in agreement with theory. The simulation indicates further that *ceteris paribus,* there will be a relative expansion in firms with intermediate product purchases concentrated in the import competing sector where prices are expected to fall in free trade. This also agrees with theory. On the other hand, producers in classifications which are actually members of the export sector have duty free access to the US market in free trade and should expand relatively in free trade. Here again the simulation is in accord with theory.

The results of the simulation are further corroborated in part two of this book where the variables introduced in this chapter are studied on a sector by sector basis. The evidence of part two supports the hypothesis that the tariff has not had the expected effect of increasing end product production in Canada. With the exception of textiles, chemicals, and food and agriculture, there would be a general shift toward end product production in free trade.

The cost of the tariff is estimated by determining the additional output that could be produced if both tariffs were eliminated. Under free trade, four per cent more of consumer goods or nine per cent more of investment goods could be made available through international specialization and exchange alone. The gains are possible without utilizing alternate technology or taking advantage of economies of scale. The estimated gain, therefore, is a conservative estimate. Considerably larger estimates are obtained when economies of scale are taken into account. Given this cost[13] and considering that the tariff has not really succeeded in protecting end stage processing, it would appear that there is a need in Canada to reconsider the role of the tariff in terms of national objectives.

2

Logical basis of this study

The logical structure of this study is founded upon certain assumptions concerning prices. These assumptions have already been discussed verbally in chapter one, but it will be necessary to amplify that discussion in this chapter. The first and second section below are concerned with this objective. The remainder of this chapter is devoted to a discussion of the implications of these assumptions. As we will show in the latter part of this chapter, the price assumptions are equivalent to the solution of a linear programming minimization problem and, therefore, imply optimization of a primal problem in which the amount of household consumption is maximized. These circumstances provide a basis for interpretation of the input-output and tariff data discussed in chapter three. A list of notation will be found in the appendix.

ASSUMPTIONS CONCERNING INTERNAL AND
EXTERNAL PRICES[1]

Under conditions of competitive equilibrium, we may assume that the prices of all commodities in the home nation (which we call nation one) have adjusted to relative prices in the rest of the world (which we call nation two) in such a way as to eliminate any inducement for traders to expand exports of any commodity or initiate new exports of commodities which are not at present exported. It follows that the price of each commodity in nation one must be greater than or equal to the price in nation two less the tariff in nation two. This condition can be expressed as

$$p_{1j} \geqslant rp_{2j} - rs_{2j} \quad \text{(all } j\text{)}, \tag{2.1}$$

where p_{1j} is the price in nation one, p_{2j} is the price in nation two, s_{2j} is the specific tariff in nation two and r is the exchange rate. If exports of commodity j

are at zero level, this condition must hold as a weak inequality. As long as the weak inequality holds, traders receive at least as much in the home nation as they do abroad. On the other hand, if commodity j is exported at any positive level, condition (2.1) must hold as an equality in equilibrium. An inequality would provide an inducement for traders to expand exports because a higher revenue would then be possible abroad. It is implicit in the assumption of competitive equilibrium that the weak inequality holds for goods that are not exported and that the equality holds for goods which are exported.

A similar condition holds with regard to the imports of nation one (exports of nation two) for precisely the same reasons. Thus,

$$rp_{2j} \geqslant p_{1j} - s_{1j} \quad \text{(all } j\text{)}, \tag{2.2}$$

where s_{1j} is the specific tariff in nation one. The weak inequality holds for all commodities which are not imported, but, in the case of goods for which there are some positive level imports, the equality must hold as in the case of constraint (2.1).

For goods which are neither exported nor imported the weak inequality must hold in both constraints (2.1) and (2.2). Producers in nation one find that they receive a price for commodity j in their own market which is at least as high as the price in nation two less the tariff in nation two. Similarly, nation two producers find that the price they can get for commodity j is at least as high in their home market as is the price in nation one less the tariff in nation one. Conditions (2.1) and (2.2) together imply

$$rs_{2j} \geqslant rp_{2j} - p_{1j} \geqslant s_{1j} \quad (j \in D), \tag{2.3}$$

where D is the set of all domestic goods. Considering the discussion of the paragraphs above, we can also write,

$$rs_{2j} = rp_{2j} - p_{1j} \quad (j \in E), \tag{2.4}$$

where E is the set of commodities j which are exported from nation one. Furthermore,

$$-s_{1j} = rp_{2j} - p_{1j} \quad (j \in M), \tag{2.5}$$

where M is the set of commodities j which are imported.

In empirical applications of the theory of effective protection and in most of the theoretical work, equality (2.5) is assumed to hold for all commodities. The equality (2.4) receives only scant attention from theorists and no attention at all in empirical applications. On the other hand, the inequalities (2.3) are entirely ignored by both. With regard to pricing behaviour, the assumptions adopted in this project are less restrictive than those needed in applications of the theory of effective protection.

In the case of goods actually imported and exported, (2.4) and (2.5) suggest a simple calculation which can be used to determine the difference between the price in nation one and the price in nation two. For imported goods the difference is equal to the tariff in nation one with a negative sign attached; for exported goods, the difference is equal to the tariff in nation two times the exchange rate. If commodity j is neither exported nor imported, however, it is free to vary as indicated by inequality (2.3). Within this range the price in nation one is determined by local conditions of supply and demand and has no fixed relationship to international prices. Outside this range there will be incentives for traders to either export or import. Over a substantial range of price, however, no such incentives will exist. A ten per cent *ad valorem* tariff in both nations, for example, would leave a possible range for variations in price equal to twenty per cent.

INTERNAL PRICE RELATIONSHIPS

It is a further consequence of the assumption of competitive equilibrium that the difference between revenue and cost (which includes wages of management and a return on capital) must be zero for processes which are used and negative or zero for any process which is not used. This assumption can be explicitly expressed as follows:

$$\sum_i p_{1i} a_{ij} + \sum_i p_{1k} b_{kj} + t_{1j} \geq p_{1j} \quad \text{(all } j\text{)}. \tag{2.6}$$

In this expression a_{ij} is the amount of the ith commodity needed to produce one unit of the jth commodity, b_{kj} is the amount of the kth resource needed to produce one unit of the jth commodity, and t_{1j} is the specific tax per unit of the jth process. If the jth process is actually used, revenue equals cost and the equality must hold in relationship (2.6). Thus

$$\sum_i p_{1i} a_{ij} + \sum_k p_{1k} b_{kj} + t_{1j} = p_{1j} \quad (j \epsilon X), \tag{2.7}$$

where X is the set of processes actually used in equilibrium. In the theory of effective protection (2.6) is assumed to hold as an equality as in (2.7). In the linear programming approach adopted in this book, we need assume only that weak inequality holds.

PRICE DETERMINATION IN EQUILIBRIUM

The constraints introduced thus far are sufficient for determining prices in nation one. The use of constraints (2.4), (2.5), and (2.7) for this purpose is most easily visualized in the context of an example. Table 2.1 illustrates the structure of the model for the case of eight commodities. It is assumed that only the first six are produced in Canada. The coefficients a_{ij} and b_{kj} in expression (2.7) appear in the first six columns of Table 2.1. For the moment, we will ignore the remaining columns. Define the column vectors ρ and ξ_B

$$\rho' = (p_{11}, p_{12}, ..., p_{1,12}, r),$$ (2.8)

$$\xi_B' = (-t_{11}, ..., -t_{16}, 0, 0, -s_{15}, -s_{16}, -s_{17}, -s_{18}, 1 -s_w).$$ (2.9)

The reader will note that the vector ξ_B' is merely the set of coefficients under the line in Table 2.1. Let Γ_B be a matrix which has elements corresponding to the coefficients above the line in Table 2.1. Considering the way that Γ_B is constructed, it is possible to verify that

$$\xi_B' = \rho' \Gamma_B.$$ (2.10)

When ρ' premultiplies one of the first six columns of Γ_B we obtain relationships (2.7). This merely expresses the assumption that the first six commodities are produced in nation one. Under conditions of equilibrium, cost must equal revenue. When ρ' premultiplies either the seventh or eighth columns of Γ_B [which in Table 2.1 are headed 'Exports of (3) and (4)'] relationships (2.4) are obtained. This multiplication, therefore, expresses the equilibrium condition implicit in the assumption that commodity three and four are exported. The price in nation two less the price in nation one equals the duty in nation two.

A similar result is obtained when ρ' multiplies column 9, 10, 11, or 12 of matrix Γ_B. When the price of vector ρ' premultiplies column 9 of Γ_B [which is the column of Table 2.1 headed 'Competing imports (5)'] the conditions (2.5) are obtained. This merely reflects the competitive equilibrium assumption that commodity five is imported. The price in nation two less the price in nation one equals the negative of the tariff in nation one. When columns 10, 11, or 12 are premultiplied by ρ' we get the same result. Commodity six is assumed to be imported as are commodities seven and eight. Since there is no production of commodity seven or eight in nation one, we refer to these as non-competing imports.

The last column of Γ_B and the last column of Table 2.1 is a retailing activity which has not yet been discussed. Goods are assumed to be sold in packages

TABLE 2.1

Example of the matrix Γ_B with eight industries

	Industry						Exports of commodity		Competing imports of commodity		Non-competing imports of commodity		Consumption
	(1)	(2)	(3)	(4)	(5)	(6)	(3)	(4)	(5)	(6)	(7)	(8)	
Commodity 1	$(-1+a_{11})$	a_{12}	a_{13}	a_{14}	a_{15}	a_{16}	0	0	0	0	0	0	w_1
Commodity 2	a_{21}	$(-1+a_{22})$	a_{23}	a_{24}	a_{25}	a_{26}	0	0	0	0	0	0	w_2
Commodity 3	a_{31}	a_{32}	$(-1+a_{33})$	a_{34}	a_{35}	a_{36}	1	0	0	0	0	0	w_3
Commodity 4	a_{41}	a_{42}	a_{43}	$(-1+a_{44})$	a_{45}	a_{46}	0	1	0	0	0	0	w_4
Commodity 5	a_{51}	a_{52}	a_{53}	a_{54}	$(-1+a_{55})$	a_{56}	0	0	-1	0	0	0	w_5
Commodity 6	a_{61}	a_{62}	a_{63}	a_{64}	a_{65}	$(-1+a_{66})$	0	0	0	-1	0	0	w_6
Commodity 7	a_{71}	a_{72}	a_{73}	a_{74}	a_{75}	a_{76}	0	0	0	0	-1	0	w_7
Commodity 8	a_{81}	a_{82}	a_{83}	a_{84}	a_{85}	a_{86}	0	0	0	0	0	-1	w_8
Resource 1	b_{11}	b_{12}	b_{13}	b_{14}	b_{15}	b_{16}	0	0	0	0	0	0	0
Resource 2	b_{21}	b_{22}	b_{23}	b_{24}	b_{25}	b_{26}	0	0	0	0	0	0	0
Resource 3	b_{31}	b_{32}	b_{33}	b_{34}	b_{35}	b_{36}	0	0	0	0	0	0	0
Resource 4	b_{41}	b_{42}	b_{43}	b_{44}	b_{45}	b_{46}	0	0	0	0	0	0	0
Balance of trade	0	0	0	0	0	0	$(-p_{23}+s_{23})$	$(-p_{24}+s_{24})$	p_{25}	p_{26}	p_{27}	p_{28}	0
	$-t_{11}$	$-t_{12}$	$-t_{13}$	$-t_{14}$	$-t_{15}$	$-t_{16}$	0	0	$-s_{15}$	$-s_{16}$	$-s_{17}$	$-s_{18}$	$1-s_w$

containing w_i of commodity i. When the price vector ρ' premultiplies this column we obtain

$$\sum_{i=1}^{N} p_{1i} w_i + s_w = 1, \tag{2.11}$$

where s_w is the sales tax. The price of the bundle of goods appearing on the left is arbitrarily set at unity and serves as the numeraire in the model. The equality in expression (2.11) holds because the cost including the sales tax of the bundle of goods sold to consumers must equal its price. The bundle of goods defined by the w_i are called the composite commodity.

For reasons which will be explained below, it is assumed that Γ_B is square and of full rank. If this is the case, Γ_B may be inverted and prices are then expressed as a function of tariffs and taxes. Thus, from (2.10),

$$\rho' = \xi_B' \Gamma_B^{-1}. \tag{2.12}$$

THE LEVEL OF NET PROTECTION

Columns one through six of the matrix Γ_B represent processes which are actually used in nation one. Commodities one and two are domestic goods whose prices are free to vary (as noted in relationship (2.3)) within the limits set by the tariffs in nation one and two. Commodities three and four are exported and the prices of these commodities, according to relationship (2.4) must be lower in nation one than in nation two by the amount of the tariff in nation two. A firm located in nation one and using commodity three or four as intermediate product has the advantage of the lower cost of these goods as compared to their cost in nation two. On the other hand, nation one imports commodities five, six, seven and eight and the price of these goods, according to relationship (2.5) must be higher in nation one by the amount of the tariff in nation one. At various points in the text we refer to this as antiprotection. A firm located in nation one and using commodities five, six, seven, and eight as intermediate inputs has a cost disadvantage due to the tariff, as compared to nation two.

The net outcome of these opposing effects can be analysed systematically by using the price relationships established in the previous sections. Let L_{1j} be the amounts paid to resource owners in nation one per unit of output:

$$L_{1j} = (p_{1j} - t_{1j}) - \sum_i p_{1i} a_{ij}. \tag{2.13}$$

If this same process were used in nation two, the amount accruing to resource owners would be L_{2j} where

$$L_{2j} = (rp_{2j} - rt_{2j}) - \sum_i rp_{2i} a_{ij}. \tag{2.14}$$

Subtracting expression (2.14) from (2.13), we obtain, using (2.4) and (2.5),

$$L_{0j} = L_{1j} - L_{2j} = S_{0j} + L_0{}^M + L_{0j}{}^E + T_{0j}, \tag{2.15}$$

where

$$S_{0j} = p_{1j} - rp_{2j}, \tag{2.16}$$

$$L_{0j}{}^E = \sum_E rs_{2i} a_{ij}, \tag{2.17}$$

$$L_{0j}{}^M = -\sum_M s_{1i} a_{ij}, \tag{2.18}$$

$$L_{0j}{}^D = -\sum_D (p_{1i} - rp_{2i}) a_{ij}, \tag{2.19}$$

$$T_{0j} = -(t_{1j} - rt_{2j}). \tag{2.20}$$

If L_{0j} is positive, tariffs and taxes favour nation one as a location for the jth process. The notation adopted helps to isolate the various reasons for differences in cost advantage due to the tariff. Of these S_{0j} is, perhaps, most obvious. The sign of S_{0j} will depend on whether commodity j is imported or exported. If commodity j is imported into nation one, S_{0j} is positive by relationship (2.5). If commodity j is exported S_{0j} is negative by relationship (2.4). If commodity j is domestic, the sign of S_{0j} depends on the relative levels of supply and demand in nation one as compared to nation two. S_{0j} is a partial equilibrium measure of the direct effect of the home and foreign tariff. The sign of S_{0j} depends on whether or not commodity j is imported or exported and its magnitude depends on the magnitude of the Canadian or US tariff whichever is relevant. The term $L_{0j}{}^M$ measures the amount that intermediate goods purchased from the import competing sector are more expensive in nation one than in nation two due to the tariff in nation one, that is, the amount of antiprotection. The term $L_{0j}{}^E$, on the other hand, measures the amount that intermediate goods purchased from the export sector of nation one are cheaper in nation one due to the foreign tariff. In the tables of part two the sum $L_{0j}{}^M + L_{0j}{}^E$ is called the cost effect per dollar of output. The term $L_{0j}{}^D$ measures the amount that intermediate goods purchased from the domestic sector cost more or less in nation one due to local differences in supply and demand in nation one compared to nation two. In general, the terms in expression (2.19) will be self-cancelling and, hence $L_{0j}{}^D$ will be small. The term T_{0j} is the amount that manufacturing taxes differ in the two nations. In this study we are concerned only with the direct plus indirect effect of the tariff on costs as measured by $S_{0j} + L_{0j}{}^M + L_{0j}{}^E$. The sum of these is a partial equilibrium measure of the cost advantage due to the tariff of processes which are actually used in Canada. The calculated magnitudes hold for given levels of the tariff as long as we may assume that commodities designated as importable, exportable or domestic do not change roles. Importable commodities must remain importable, exportable remain exportable and domestic commodities must remain domestic. Consequently, this type of cost data must be examined with great care and must always be studied in conjunction with the more general simulation approach presented below.

PRODUCTION RELATIONSHIPS

The preceding sections established certain price relationships. It is now necessary to turn to a number of production relationships which play an important part in the simulation used in this study. Let x_j be the amount of the jth commodity produced in nation one, e_j be the amount of the jth commodity exported from nation one, m_j the amount of the jth commodity imported into nation one, and y be the number of units of the composite commodity (defined by (2.11)) demanded in equilibrium. Furthermore, let $\mathbf{x}_B$ be the vector where

$$\mathbf{x}_B{}' = (x_1, ..., x_6, e_3, e_4, m_5, ..., m_8, y), \tag{2.21}$$

and let the vector ζ be defined as

$$\zeta' = (-g_1, ..., -g_8, z_1, ..., z_5).$$

The first eight components of ζ are the levels of government demand for commodities one through eight. The next four components of ζ are the supplies of resources nine through twelve. The last component of ζ is the change in the stock of foreign exchange. If there are N commodities and R resources, the first N components of ζ would have negative signs attached. In equilibrium

$$\zeta = \Gamma_B \mathbf{x}_B. \tag{2.22}$$

By referring to Table 2.1 it is readily verified that equation (2.22) is merely the equilibrium condition that supply equals demand. When the vector $\mathbf{x}_B$ postmultiplies the first row of Γ_B we obtain $-x_1 + \Sigma a_{1j}x_j + w_1 y = -g_1$, which, after rearranging, becomes

$$g_1 + \sum_{j=1}^{6} a_{1j}x_j + w_1 y = x_1.$$

On the left hand side of this expression there are three sources of demand. The first term, g_1, is the exogenously determined government demand. The second term, $\sum a_{1j}x_j$, is the demand for commodity j as an intermediate commodity in production. The third term $w_1 y$ is the demand for commodity one by households. The amount supplied is x_1. Since commodity one is domestic, none is demanded for export or supplied as an import.

The situation with regard to commodity three is only slightly different. When x_B post-multiplies row three we obtain

$$g_3 + \sum_{j=1}^{6} a_{3j}x_j + e_3 + w_3 y = x_3.$$

Since commodity three is exported, e_3 appears on the left as an additional source of demand. In the case of commodity five, nation one is assumed to be an importer. When x_B multiplies row five, we obtain,

$$g_5 + \sum_{j=1}^{6} a_{5j}x_j + w_5 y = x_5 + m_5.$$

In this case m_5 appears on the right as an additional source of supply. In each case, the first eight equations obtained from relationship (2.22) reflect the assumption that there is an equilibrium in the supply and demand for some commodity. In the general case this will be true for the first N equations.

Resource supply and demand is expressed by equations 9 through 12 of equations (2.22). For example, when x_B multiplies row 9 we obtain

$$\sum_{j=1}^{6} b_{1j}x_j = z_1.$$

In this case, z_1 is the fixed supply of resource one and the demand for resource one appears on the left. There are R resource constraints.

When x_B multiplies the last row of Γ_B we obtain the thirteenth equation of the system:

$$\sum_{j=5}^{8} m_j p_{2j} = (p_{23} - s_{23}) e_3 + (p_{24} - s_{24}) e_4 + z_5. \tag{2.23}$$

The term on the left is the amount of foreign exchange demanded for the purpose of purchasing imports. On the right, the first two terms are the foreign exchange supplied indirectly through the sale of exports, and z_5 is the amount of foreign exchange supplied out of reserves plus net capital flows.

Since, for reasons discussed below, Γ_B is assumed to be square and of full rank, we can obtain the inverse relationship

$$x_B = \Gamma_B^{-1}\zeta. \tag{2.24}$$

The components of the vector x_B are the industrial output levels and levels of imports and exports and of the composite commodity. These are determined by ζ whose components give the exogenous levels of government expenditure and the fixed supply of resources. For sufficiently small changes in the components of ζ producers will not be induced to change from one process to another and the elements of Γ_B and hence of Γ_B^{-1} can be regarded as a set of constants; thus from expression (2.24)

$$\partial y \mathbin{/} \partial g_i = -q_{ni} \qquad (i = 1, ..., N),$$

$$\partial y \mathbin{/} \partial z_k = q_{nh} \qquad (h = N + k; k = 1, ..., R), \tag{2.25}$$

$$\partial y \mathbin{/} \partial z_n = q_{nn},$$

where N is the number of commodities and R is the number of resources and $n = N + R + 1$. The coefficients q_{nh} are elements in the last row of Γ_B^{-1}. The element q_{nh} may be interpreted as the change in the output of the composite commodity obtained from a unit increase in the supply of commodity i, resource k, or unit of foreign exchange. In the case of commodities, the extra supply comes from the reduced purchases of government. In the case of resources, it comes from an increase in the supply of resource k. Increases in foreign exchange, must come from the planned reduction in the stock of foreign exchange. Irrespective of which of these is assumed to change, the associated change in the composite commodity depends on the potential of the economy for absorbing an extra unit in production and the over-all prospects of converting any increased output into units of the composite commodity. Since goods are assumed to be absorbed in fixed proportions, consumption must increase in fixed proportions. If production is not increased in exactly the required proportion, a correctly proportioned aggregate consumption must be obtained through an international exchange of production in excess supply domestically for goods whose domestic production has not sufficiently increased.

GENERAL EQUILIBRIUM RELATIONSHIP BETWEEN
TAXES AND PRICES

At this point it is helpful to write out relationship (2.12) in more detailed form. Recalling definition (2.8) and (2.9), we obtain from equation (2.12)

$$p_{1h} = -\sum_{i=1}^{6} t_{1i}q_{ih} - \sum_{i=9}^{12} s_{1,i-4}q_{ih} - s_w q_{nh} + q_{nh} \quad (h = 1, ..., N+R),$$

$$r = -\sum_{i=1}^{6} t_{1i}q_{in} - \sum_{i=9}^{12} s_{1,i-4}q_{in} - s_w q_{nn} + q_{nn}. \tag{2.26}$$

Because of relationship (2.25), if all taxes and tariffs are zero the expressions (2.26) can be reduced to

$$p_{1i} = q_{ni} = -\partial y / \partial g_i \qquad (i = 1, ..., N),$$

$$p_{1h} = q_{nh} = \partial y / \partial z_k \qquad (h = N+k; k = 1, ..., R), \tag{2.27}$$

$$r = q_{nn} = \partial y / \partial z_n.$$

In free trade, with all taxes and tariffs equal to zero, the prices of each commodity in equilibrium and the exchange rate are equal to their incremental value in production as defined in expression (2.25). Since neither p_{1h} nor r can be negative in equilibrium, it follows that q_{nh} are all positive or zero. Furthermore, from (2.27),

$$(\partial y / \partial g_i) / p_{1i} = (\partial y / \partial z_k) / p_{1h} = (\partial y / \partial z_n) / r = 1. \tag{2.28}$$

Per dollar of domestic currency, the incremental increase in any commodity, resource or foreign exchange produces the same amount of the composite commodity, therefore each such ratio is equal to every other. This is a necessary condition for maximizing the amount of the composite commodity. If it were not true, it would be possible to increase the amount of the composite commodity produced by reducing the use of resources (or commodities or the unit of foreign exchange) in processes where the incremental effect per dollar of output is low and using more in processes where production per dollar of output is higher. Condition (2.28) is violated if any taxes or tariffs are present and, therefore the marginal conditions necessary for optimality fail. The price of the factor of production is no longer equal to its incremental value in production.

LINEAR PROGRAMMING FORMULATION

The reader will have recognized by this point that the coefficients of Table 2.1 are part of a standard programming format which can be explicitly stated in cannonical form. Maximize

$$u = -\sum_{j=1}^{N} t_{1j}x_j - \sum_{j=1}^{N} s_{1j}m_j + (1 - s_w)y, \qquad (2.29)$$

subject to

$$-x_i + \sum_{j=1}^{N} a_{ij}x_j + e_i - m_i + w_iy + d_i = -g_i \quad (i = 1, ..., N), \qquad (2.30)$$

$$\sum_{j=1}^{N} b_{kj}x_j + d_k = z_k \quad (k = 1, ..., R), \qquad (2.31)$$

$$-\sum_{j=1}^{N} (p_{2j} - s_{2j})e_j + \sum_{j=1}^{N} p_{2j}m_j + d_n = z_n = 0, \qquad (2.32)$$

and

$$x_j, e_j, m_j, d_i, d_k, d_n, y \geqslant 0. \qquad (2.33)$$

All notation has been defined previously except the d's. The d_i represent the excess supply of commodity i, the d_k represent the excess supply of resource k, and d_n is the excess supply of foreign exchange (balance of trade surplus). Each of these must be non-negative to satisfy the feasibility condition that the amounts of commodity i, resource k, or foreign exchange used cannot exceed the amount made available. Furthermore, it is not inconsistent with our equilibrium assumptions if either d_i or d_k is greater than zero. If, for example, the price of commodity i falls to zero, we may have an equilibrium in which supply exceeds demand and hence d_i will be positive. It is assumed, however, that the exchange rate never falls to zero and hence that the amount of foreign exchange supplied is equal to the amount demanded. This implies that $d_n = 0$. For expositional convenience, we also assume that the government does not wish to increase or decrease its stock of foreign exchange and that net capital flows are zero. Therefore, $z_n = 0$.

The structure of the model is illustrated in Table 2.2 where the detached coefficient form of the primal problem for the case $N = 8$ and $R = 4$ is shown. (The slack activities for the d's are omitted.) The tableau shown in Table 2.2 should be compared to Table 2.1. The matrix of coefficients in Table 2.2 is denoted Γ. The matrix of coefficients from Table 2.1 is denoted Γ_B because it is assumed to be the optimal basic matrix selected from Γ. This is the rationale for our earlier assumption that Γ_B is square and of full rank. It is also readily verified from Table 2.2 that it is formally unnecessary to assume that each commodity is produced from only one process. By adding columns to Γ it would be possible to introduce alternative processes for each commodity. This would increase the number of columns of Γ without changing the number of rows.

For the exposition below, it is convenient to have the primal problem in vector-matrix notation. Let $\mathbf{x}$ be a vector whose components are the activity levels of the primal problem. The first N components of $\mathbf{x}$ are the production activity levels x_j and the next N components of $\mathbf{x}$ are the export activity levels e_j. Following these are N components of import activities m_j followed again by N components d_j, R components d_k and d_n. The last component of $\mathbf{x}$ is the retailing activity y. In order to refer to the components of $\mathbf{x}$ generally we denote these v_h. Let ξ be a vector whose components appear as coefficients in the objective function, and recall that ζ is a vector whose components appear as constants on the right hand side of the primal problem. We may, therefore, state the primal problem in matrix-vector notation. Maximize

$$u = \xi'\mathbf{x}, \tag{2.34}$$

subject to

$$\Gamma\mathbf{x} = \zeta \tag{2.35}$$

$$\mathbf{x} \geqslant 0. \tag{2.36}$$

The price relationships discussed in the first section of this chapter apply to the dual of the primal problem. Let p_{1h} and r be the dual variables. The dual problem is to minimize

$$u_{min} = -\sum_{i=1}^{N} p_{1i}g_i + \sum_{k=1}^{R} p_{1k}z_k + rz_n, \tag{2.37}$$

subject to

$$-p_{1j} + \sum_{i=1}^{N} p_{1i}a_{ij} + \sum_{k=1}^{R} p_{1k}b_{kj} \geqslant -t_{1j} \quad (j = 1, ..., N), \tag{2.38}$$

$$p_{1j} - r(p_{2j} - s_{2j}) \geqslant 0 \quad (j = 1, ..., N), \tag{2.39}$$

$$-p_{1j} + rp_{2j} \geqslant -s_{1j} \quad (j = 1, ..., N), \tag{2.40}$$

$$p_{1i}, p_{1k}, r \geqslant 0, \tag{2.41}$$

$$\sum_{i=1}^{N} p_{1i}w_i \geqslant 1 - s_w. \tag{2.42}$$

TABLE 2.2

Detached coefficient form of the example primal problem

	Industry								Exports of Commodity		
	(1)	(2)	(3)	(4)	(5)	(6)	(7)	(8)	(1)	(2)	(3)
Commodity 1	$(-1+a_{11})$	a_{12}	a_{13}	a_{14}	a_{15}	a_{16}	a_{17}	a_{18}	1	0	0
Commodity 2	a_{21}	$(-1+a_{22})$	a_{23}	a_{24}	a_{25}	a_{26}	a_{27}	a_{28}	0	1	0
Commodity 3	a_{31}	a_{32}	$(-1+a_{33})$	a_{34}	a_{35}	a_{36}	a_{37}	a_{38}	0	0	1
Commodity 4	a_{41}	a_{42}	a_{43}	$(-1+a_{44})$	a_{45}	a_{46}	a_{47}	a_{48}	0	0	0
Commodity 5	a_{51}	a_{52}	a_{53}	a_{54}	$(-1+a_{55})$	a_{56}	a_{57}	a_{58}	0	0	0
Commodity 6	a_{61}	a_{62}	a_{63}	a_{64}	a_{65}	$(-1+a_{66})$	a_{67}	a_{68}	0	0	0
Commodity 7	a_{71}	a_{72}	a_{73}	a_{74}	a_{75}	a_{76}	$(-1+a_{77})$	a_{78}	0	0	0
Commodity 8	a_{81}	a_{82}	a_{83}	a_{84}	a_{85}	a_{86}	a_{87}	$(-1+a_{88})$	0	0	0
Resource 1	b_{11}	b_{12}	b_{13}	b_{14}	b_{15}	b_{16}	b_{17}	b_{18}	0	0	0
Resource 2	b_{21}	b_{22}	b_{23}	b_{24}	b_{25}	b_{26}	b_{27}	b_{28}	0	0	0
Resource 3	b_{31}	b_{32}	b_{33}	b_{34}	b_{35}	b_{36}	b_{37}	b_{38}	0	0	0
Resource 4	b_{41}	b_{42}	b_{43}	b_{44}	b_{45}	b_{46}	b_{47}	b_{48}	0	0	0
Balance of trade	0	0	0	0	0	0	0	0	$(-p_{21}+s_{21})$	$(-p_{22}+s_{22})$	$(-p_{23}+s_{23})$
	$-t_{11}$	$-t_{12}$	$-t_{13}$	$-t_{14}$	$-t_{15}$	$-t_{16}$	$-t_{17}$	$-t_{18}$	0	0	0

TABLE 2.2 continued

	Exports of Commodity					Imports of Commodity								Consumption
	(4)	(5)	(6)	(7)	(8)	(1)	(2)	(3)	(4)	(5)	(6)	(7)	(8)	
Commodity 1	0	0	0	0	0	-1	0	0	0	0	0	0	0	w_1
Commodity 2	0	0	0	0	0	0	-1	0	0	0	0	0	0	w_2
Commodity 3	0	0	0	0	0	0	0	-1	0	0	0	0	0	w_3
Commodity 4	1	0	0	0	0	0	0	0	-1	0	0	0	0	w_4
Commodity 5	0	1	0	0	0	0	0	0	0	-1	0	0	0	w_5
Commodity 6	0	0	1	0	0	0	0	0	0	0	-1	0	0	w_6
Commodity 7	0	0	0	1	0	0	0	0	0	0	0	-1	0	w_7
Commodity 8	0	0	0	0	1	0	0	0	0	0	0	0	-1	w_8
Resource 1	0	0	0	0	0	0	0	0	0	0	0	0	0	0
Resource 2	0	0	0	0	0	0	0	0	0	0	0	0	0	0
Resource 3	0	0	0	0	0	0	0	0	0	0	0	0	0	0
Resource 4	0	0	0	0	0	0	0	0	0	0	0	0	0	0
Balance of trade	$(-p_{24}+s_{24})$	$(-p_{25}+s_{25})$	$(-p_{26}+s_{26})$	$(-p_{27}+s_{27})$	$(-p_{28}+s_{28})$	p_{21}	p_{22}	p_{23}	p_{24}	p_{25}	p_{26}	p_{27}	p_{28}	0
	0	0	0	0	0	$-s_{11}$	$-s_{12}$	$-s_{13}$	$-s_{14}$	$-s_{15}$	$-s_{16}$	$-s_{17}$	$-s_{18}$	$1-s_W$

In the canonical form of the linear programming problem, the dual variables are unrestricted in sign. Nevertheless, the reader may verify (by observing the outcome when ρ' multiplies the disposal activities of Γ) that, condition (2.41) must hold in the dual. We shall also want to express the dual in the matrix-vector form. Minimize

$$u_{min} = \rho'\varsigma$$

subject to

$$\rho'\Gamma \geqslant \xi' \tag{2.43}$$

and

$$\rho' \geqslant 0. \tag{2.44}$$

SIMULATED LEVELS OF TRADE

The solution to the primal problem constitutes a simulation of the actual conditions of production and trade under competitive conditions. If, for example, the 1961 levels of output, exports, imports, and relative prices and the exchange rate were unknown, these could be determined by finding the solution to the primal and dual problems. We will prove this proposition in this section because it has two important applications in this study.

First of all, it offers an opportunity to check the numerical accuracy of the data. When actual 1961 taxes and tariffs are assigned as values for t_{1j}, s_{2j}, and s_{2j}, the solution to the primal problem and the dual should correspond to the actual levels of output, exports, imports, relative prices, and the exchange rate observed in 1961. Secondly, the proposition proved in this section justifies the use of the problem format as a simulation. By setting all tariffs and taxes at zero, we obtain a simulated version of the actual conditions of free trade.

The proof follows directly from the mathematics of linear programming.[2] Let ρ_0 be the price vector observed in competitive equilibrium and let x be any vector whatever which is feasible in the primal problem. Since ρ_0 is feasible in the dual, it follows from constraints (2.34), (2.35), (2.36), (2.43), and (2.44) that

$$\rho_0'\varsigma = \rho_0'\Gamma x \geqslant \xi'x = u. \tag{2.45}$$

A condition similar to expression (2.45) holds for the equilibrium activity vector. Let $v_h{}^0$ be the hth activity level in competitive equilibrium and let x_0 be a vector with components $v_h{}^0$. Furthermore, let x_B be a vector whose components are the non-zero activity levels $v_h{}^0$. We refer to either $\mathbf{x}_0$ or $\mathbf{x}_B$ as the equilibrium activity vector. Let Γ_B be a matrix of those activity vectors for which $v_h{}^0 > 0$ and let ξ_B be those components of ξ for which $v_h{}^0 > 0$. In the example, $\mathbf{x}_B$ was defined by expression (2.21), ξ_B by equation (2.9), and Γ_B was illustrated by Table 2.1. As we explained in the opening section of this chapter, the equilibrium price vector satisfies the constraints (2.4), (2.5), and (2.7). Therefore, equality (2.10) holds, and using (2.22) we obtain

$$\rho_0{}'\zeta = \rho_0{}'\Gamma_B \mathbf{x}_B = \xi_B{}'\mathbf{x}_B = u^0. \tag{2.46}$$

By substituting $\rho_0{}'\zeta$ on the left of (2.45) it is clear that $u^0 \geqslant u$. The equilibrium activity vector $\mathbf{x}_B$ gives at least as large a value to the objective function as any other feasible solution to the primal problem.

It is one of the mathematical properties of linear programming that the optimal solution of the primal problem must equal the optimal solution of the dual problem. Using this property we can verify an aggregate equilibrium condition. From expressions (2.29) and (2.37),

$$\sum_{k=1}^{R} p_{1k} z_k + \sum_{j=1}^{N} t_{1j} x_j + \sum_{j=1}^{N} s_{1j} m_j + s_w y = r z_n +$$
$$\sum_{i=1}^{N} p_{1i} g_i + y. \tag{2.47}$$

On the left of expression (2.47) we find income plus taxes (*including* tariff revenue). On the right we find net imports plus government spending and consumption. This demonstrates an additional advantage of the general equilibrium approach over the partial equilibrium methods which characterize the theory of effective protection. The general equilibrium model satisfies the condition that aggregate income (measured as value added) must equal the value of goods produced.

Perhaps some statement is in order concerning the role of investment in aggregate demand. For expositional simplicity we have defined the g_i $(i = 1, ..., N)$ as government spending. When dealing with the actual data, the g_i represent both private investment and government spending. This feature can be introduced formally into the model if we let $g_i{}'$ be private investment and $g_i{}''$ be government spending on commodity i. Substitute $g_i = g_i{}' + g_i{}''$ in expression (2.47). Investment now will appear explicitly as $\Sigma\, p_{1i} g_i{}'$ and government spending as $\Sigma\, p_{1i} g_i{}''$.

OPTIMAL USE OF RESOURCES[3]

Let us refer to the situation where some of the t_{1j}, s_{1j}, or s_{2j} are greater than zero as the restricted trade situation, and let us refer to the situation where all tariffs and taxes are equal to zero as the free trade situation. The value of the composite commodity in the restricted trade situation is determined by maximizing the primal problem described by constraints (2.29) through (2.33). In the previous section we proved that this maximization occurs as a consequence of market forces. It does not follow, however, that maximizing u will maximize the index of welfare. The amount of the composite commodity available depends solely on the value of y. From inspection of the objective function (2.29), it can be seen that the primal problem does not maximize y unless all tariffs and taxes are equal to zero. When tariffs and taxes are at levels different from zero, market forces act in such a way as to maximize u rather than y. In free trade, however, u and y are the same and, as we will show below, the value of y in free trade is greater than in any other situation.

To prove the point, we shall show that the solution to the restricted trade problem can always be made feasible (but not necessarily optimal) in the free trade problem format but that the free trade solution is not feasible in the restricted trade problem format. It follows that free trade must produce an amount of the composite commodity at least as large as restricted trade. Recall from chapter one that it is assumed that nation one is too small to affect relative prices in nation two. These may therefore be regarded as constants.

The problem format for the free trade situation is the same as for the restricted trade situation as far as constraints (2.30) through (2.32) are concerned but the balance of payments constraint (2.29) and the objective function will be different. Since t_{1j}, s_{1j}, s_{2j}, and s_w are all zero in free trade, constraint (2.32) has the form

$$- \sum_{j=1}^{N} p_{2j} e_j + \sum_{j=1}^{N} p_{2j} m_j + d_n = 0, \tag{2.48}$$

and the objective function will take the form

$$u = y. \tag{2.49}$$

To prove that the restricted trade solution x_0 satisfies the constraints of the free trade problem format, we merely need to prove that x_0 satisfies constraint (2.48) because every other constraint in the free trade problem is identical to a corresponding constraint in the restricted trade format. In the optimal solution for restricted trade, $m_j = m_j^0$, $e_j = e_j^0$, and $d_n = 0$. We can assign the values m_j^0 and e_j^0 to the variables in the free trade problem format without violating the constraint (2.48) provided we set $d_n = \Sigma s_{2j} e_j^0$. Since $d_n \geqslant 0$, and no other constraint is violated, the restricted solution is feasible in the free trade format.

On the other hand, the free trade solution must violate the balance of trade constraint of the restricted trade problem. Let e_j^f and m_j^f be the free trade values of these variables. Since $d_n = 0$ in equilibrium, the free trade balance of trade constraint (2.48) must hold with $e_j = e_j^f$, $m_j = m_j^f$, and $d_n = 0$. It can be seen by comparison that e_j^f and m_j^f cannot satisfy the restricted trade balance of trade constraint (2.32) unless we set $d_n = -\Sigma s_{2j} e_j^f$. But that would violate the non-negativity constraint on this variable. The free trade solution cannot earn enough foreign exchange to satisfy the restricted trade balance of trade constraint.

Since the free trade situation produces the maximum of the composite commodity, we take the output levels of free trade as the norm for purposes of ascertaining the Canadian comparative advantage.

ALTERNATIVE REVENUE SOURCES

The gains from free trade as measured by u represent real gains which accrue from the improved allocation of resources measured in units of the composite commodity. There are, implicitly, substantial losses of tax and tariff revenue but this may be recovered without reducing the gains from trade. In free trade, the sales tax can be arbitrarily set without affecting the levels of output, trade flows, or the level of the composite commodity.

Suppose we wish to change the sales tax from its level s_w^0 to a new level, $\bar{s}_w = c \, \Sigma \, w_i p_{1i}^0 + s_w^0$ where $c < 1$ is a scalar and p_{1i}^0 is the price of commodity i before the change in the sales tax. Effectively there is a new problem format in which the value of s_w^0 in (2.42) is changed to $\bar{s}_w$ and we would like to know if the old solution x_0 is optimal in the new format. It is easy to determine the appropriate simplex multipliers. If p_{1i}^0, p_{1k}^0 and r^0 are the simplex multipliers before the change in s_w, the new simplex multipliers will be $p_{1i}^* = p_{1i}^0 (1 - c)$, $p_{1k}^* = p_{1k}^0 (1 - c)$ and $r^* = r^0 (1 - c)$. From inspection of constraints (2.38) through (2.41) (recalling that $t_{1j} = s_{1j} = s_{2j} = 0$), it is clear that in any case where the equality held before s_w was changed, it must hold again after we set s_w at the value $\bar{s}_w$. It follows that p_{1i}^*, p_{1k}^* and r^* are simplex multipliers. Furthermore, in cases where the inequality held before the change in s_w, it will continue to hold after s_w is changed and hence the simplex criteria are all satisfied for the solution x_0. The level of the sales tax can be set arbitrarily without changing the equilibrium solution. The gains from free trade are not affected if the tariff revenue previously collected by the government is obtained under free trade through an increased sales tax. This is why our method of measuring the gains from free trade need not take account of the tariff revenues lost under free trade.

CONCLUDING REMARKS

There are three formulations of the linear programme as defined above. The first is the actual 1961 situation which is replicated by the model, the second is the free trade situation described above in which all tariffs and taxes are set at zero. The third formulation could be called the free trade short-run model. In this model, industrial output levels are constrained to stay within a ten per cent variation and it is assumed there is no shift in the direction of trade in any commodity. Commodities exported before the tariff reductions are not allowed to become imports after the reduction in tariffs, commodities imported before the reduction are not allowed to become exports and domestic commodities remain domestic.

The reader will be aware that this type of approach has limitations. The index of welfare is defined in terms of the 1961 pattern of consumption. These proportions will change if we shift to free trade because per capita income will change, because the distribution of income will change, and because relative prices will change. We are not able on the production side to make allowance for alternative production process or for economies of scale and we must assume that resource commodities are fixed in supply. As noted in chapter one the estimate of the cost of the tariff is therefore an understatement. In practice there will be additional gains possible from substitution in production and from economies of scale. Insofar as we regard the change in the index of welfare as a cardinal measure of the change in utility it is underestimated because it does not allow for gains in utility arising from substitutions in consumption or from adjustments in the supply of resources.

On the other hand, the method does give a proper indication of the gain that can be made through specialization and exchange. The import vector of the primal problem represents the cheapest foreign alternative available to the national economy. The US prices appearing in these vectors may be assumed to represent the cost of alternative supply under the most ideal conditions abroad. These prices reflect the advantages in technology, scale, and relative endowments of the United States. By measuring the cost of the tariff in terms of these prices, we expect to obtain a meaningful measure of the extent to which the tariff prevents Canadians from benefitting from the cheaper sources of foreign supply.

APPENDIX

List of notation

Indexes

N is the number of commodities.
R is the number of resources.
n $= N + R + 1$.
i is an index for commodities with range 1 to N.
j is used interchangeably with i.
k is an index for resources with range 1 to R.
D is the set of all domestic goods.

E is the set of all exportable goods.

M is the set of all importable goods.

X is the set of all goods produced in the home nation.

Vectors and components

ρ is an $N + R + 1$ vector with components p_{1h} in the first $N + R$ places and r in the last place.

p_{1h} for $h = j$ ($j = 1, ..., N$) is the price of the jth commodity in nation one.

p_{1h} for $h = N + k$ ($k = 1, ..., R$) is the price of the kth resource.

r is the exchange rate.

ζ is an $N + R + 1$ vector with components $-g_i$ in the first N places, z_k in the next R places, and z_n in the final place.

g_i is the sum of all exogenous demands for commodity i including government spending and changes in inventory.

z_k is the supply of resource k.

z_n is the planned change in foreign exchange reserves plus the net capital inflow.

ξ is a $3N + 1$ vector with $-t_{1j}$ in the first N places, zeroes in the next N places, $-s_{1j}$ in the next N places and $1-s_w$ in the last place.

t_{1j} is the specific manufacturing tax in nation 1 on industry j.

s_{1j} is the specific tariff in nation one on commodity j.

s_w is the sales tax.

ζ_B is an $N + R + 1$ vector with components selected from ζ. If $v_h = 0$ the hth component of ζ will be omitted from ζ_B.

$\mathbf{x}$ is a $4N + R + 2$ vector with components v_h where

v_h $= x_j$ ($j = 1, ..., N$).

v_h $= e_j$ ($h = N + j; j = 1, ..., N$).

v_h $= m_j$ ($h = 2N + j; j = 1, ..., N$).

v_h $= y$ ($h = 3N + 1$).

v_h $= d_j$ ($h = 3N + 1 + j; j = 1, ..., N$).

v_h $= d_k$ ($h = 4N + 1 + k; k = 1, ..., R$).

v_h $= d_h$ ($h = n$).

x_j is the level of output in commodity classification j.

e_j is the level of exports in commodity classification j.

m_j is the level of imports in commodity classification j.

d_j is the excess supply of commodity j.

d_k is the excess supply of resource k.

d_n is the excess supply of foreign exchange.

$\mathbf{x}_B$ is an $N + R + 1$ vector made-up of those components of x which are basic.

Matrices and elements of matrices

Γ	is an $N + R + 1$ by $4N + R + 2$ matrix of detached coefficients arranged in the manner of Table 2.2 except that we must add $N + R + 1$ disposal activities.
a_{ij}	is the number of units of the ith commodity needed to produce one unit of the jth commodity.
b_{kj}	is the number of units of the kth resource needed to produce the jth commodity.
s_{2j}	is the specific tariff in nation two on commodity j.
w_i	is the number of units of commodity i purchased per dollar spent on consumer goods.
Γ_B	is a matrix obtained by selecting columns from Γ. If v_h is basic, column h is chosen as a member of Γ_B.
q_{nh}	$(h = 1, ..., n)$ are elements in the last row of Γ_B^{-1}. The elements of Γ_B^{-1} are, in general, denoted by a doubly subscripted q.

Other notation

u	is the value of the objective function in the primal problem.
u_{min}	is the value of the objective function in the dual.
c	is an arbitrary scalar.
L_{1j}	the amount paid to resource owners in nation one per unit of output.
L_{2j}	the amount paid to resource owners in nation two per unit of output.
L_{0j}	$= L_{2j} - L_{1j}$.
S_{0j}	= the amount that the price of commodity j in nation two exceeds the price in nation one.
L_{0j}^M	measures the amount that intermediate goods purchased from the import competing sector are more expensive in nation one than in nation two.
L_{0j}^E	measures the amount that intermediate goods purchased from the export sector of nation one are cheaper in nation one than in nation two.
L_{0j}^D	measures the amount that intermediate goods purchased from the domestic sector cost more or less in nation one due to local differences in supply and demand.
T_{0j}	is the amount that manufacturing taxes in nation two exceed manufacturing taxes in nation one.
t_{2j}	is the specific manufacturing tax in nation 2 on commodity j.
p_{2j}	is the price of commodity j in nation 2.

3

Implementation and statistical organization

In the preceding chapter we described the logic behind certain numerical calculations which were to be applied to the Canadian case. Before such calculations could be made, however, it was necessary to pass through a preliminary stage of data organization in which the Canadian Input-Output Table for 1961, the Customs Tariff in Canada and the Tariff Schedule of the United States were combined into a single model. In this preliminary stage of the project a classification of commodities was determined and an estimate was made of the Canadian and US tariffs which would be assigned to each class. On the basis of these data it was then possible to prepare Tables 3.2 through 3.5 which are used in part two of this book. Some readers may feel that they have already obtained a sufficient understanding of the logical basis of this study from chapters one or two. Anyone willing to tolerate a certain degree of uncertainty about the statistical foundations may skip over to part two without loss of continuity.

The raw data used to estimate the parameters of the model are input-output commodity flows taken from tables defined at Statistics Canada according to an 189-industrial and 644-commodity classification. It was necessary to aggregate these data because it was not computationally possible to manage more than about 100 classes and because, with a larger number of classes, some cells in the flow matrix would become confidential. As a consequence of preliminary research, it was determined that a 103-level commodity classification would be most satisfactory. The relationship between the 103-level commodity code and the Statistics Canada 644-level commodity code is shown in Table 3.1. Each commodity at the 644 level of classification is itself defined in terms of the Canadian Commodity Classification, the Import Commodity Classification and the Export Commodity Classification of Statistics Canada (15-501, 1969, 187-236). The interested reader can obtain considerable detail concerning each of the 103-level groups by tracing definitions through the 644-level code on down to the various commodity codes.

THE 103-LEVEL OF CLASSIFICATION

In order to determine appropriate definitions for the 103-level of classification, the export and import levels of each commodity were first studied at the level of the Import and Export Commodity codes of Statistics Canada (65-004, 1965 and 65-007, 1965). Trade data for 1961 could not be used for this purpose however. Both the import and export commodity codes of 1961 have been superseded and the 644-level input-output classes are defined in terms of the newer commodity codes. The newer import and export commodity codes were not actually used in connection with trade data until 1964 and therefore it was necessary to base our preliminary classification decisions on the 1964 data rather than on 1961 trade flows. Trade in commodities at this level was examined in order to determine which classes were primarily exportable, which were import competing and which were primarily domestic. The criteria which seemed appropriate from the preliminary examination of trade data were then tested on the 644-level classification of trade data available from the 1961 Input-Output table.

There are few products at the 644-level of classification which are purely exports or purely imports. This is, in part, due to the heterogeneous nature of the commodity groupings at this level and in part due to the sheer length of the Canadian-US border. In cases where the transport cost, East-West, exceeds the Canadian tariff plus transport costs, North-South, goods will be imported over the Canadian tariff at some points even though they are, on the whole, commodities which are exported. The rule was adopted that no commodity group at the 644-level would be aggregated with another group at the 644-level unless trade data indicated that both were groups of exported commodities, or that both were groups of imported commodities, or that both were groups of domestic commodities. As a consequence of this preliminary work, a classification at the 103-level was obtained which satisfied three criteria. The first criterion is based on the ratio of trade to production. In all commodity groups which are designated exported commodities or imported commodities, the ratio of trade to production is at least nine per cent and most are well above this. In all groups which are designated domestic commodities, the ratio of trade to production is less than six per cent and most are well below this level. The second criterion is based on a comparison of the magnitude of exports to the magnitude of imports. The ratio of imports to exports in the case of an import class or the ratio of exports to imports in the case of an export class is in every case at least seven to one. The third criterion is based on trade with the United States. With one exception, noted below, the ratio of trade with the United States to trade with the rest of the world is at least ten per cent. This last criterion was introduced because of our assumption that the U.S. price represents the least costly foreign

TABLE 3.1

Definitions of 103-level industries according to the 644-level input-output Code[1]

Name	644-level commodity code
1 Services to agriculture, D	024
2 Services to mining, D	051
3 Meat, except fish and poultry, D	052-064
4 Poultry processed, D	065, 066
5 Dairy products, D	067-074
6 Feed meal, D	087-091
7 Cereal and bakery, D	095, 096, 098
8 Sugar refinery products, D	104, 105
9 Confectionary products, D	101, 102, 116
10 Tobacco, processed, D	126-128
11 Leather, D	144
12 Wood products, D	213, 214, 216-228
13 Iron and steel intermediates, D	262, 263, 265, 267, 270, 275, 277, 299
	301, 339, 340
14 Non-ferrous metal products, D	284-287, 292, 315, 331, 332
15 Electrical products, D	396, 400, 410, 411
16 Mineral products, D	415, 416, 418-421, 434
17 Explosives, D	446-449
18 Chemicals, D	467, 481, 483-490, 492, 493, 495, 496,
	498, 503-505, 507, 514, 515, 525, 552
19 Dressing and dyeing, D	181, 571
20 Construction, D	582
21 Transportation, D	583-595, 600, 603-607
22 Electric power, D	599
23 Water services, D	602
24 Communications, D	596-598
25 Business service, D	367, 608-611, 617, 618, 620-622, 628, 630
26 Personal service, D	612-616, 619, 623-627, 629
27 Advertising and travel, D	256, 257, 636, 637
28 Paper products, D	232-237, 240, 241, 243-250
29 Fish products, E	076
30 Flour, malt, and starch, E	092, 094, 097, 110
31 Beet, pulp, and sugar, E	103, 111
32 Wood, pulp, and Lumber, E	209-212, 215, 229-231, 238, 239, 242
33 Iron and steel intermediates, E	260, 261
34 Non-ferrous metal products, E	279-283, 288, 289, 291, 293-295, 308, 311
35 Inorganic chemicals, E	450, 453, 465, 466, 468-470, 473, 475-477,
	480, 491, 509, 516, 523
36 Liquor and beer, E	120, 121, 123, 124
37 Repair and supply service, E	631-635, 638
38 Processed foods, M	075, 077-086, 093, 099, 100, 106-109,
	112-115, 117-119
39 Alcohol and wine, M	122, 125

TABLE 3.1 cont'd.

Name	644-level commodity code
40 Rubber products, M	129-143
41 Leather products, M	145, 147-149
42 Cotton textile products, M	150-155, 167, 169, 170
43 Wool textile products, M	156-159, 168, 178, 179
44 Other textile products, M	146, 160-166, 171, 177, 180, 182-208
45 Printing, M	251-255, 258
46 Graphite and carbon, M	271, 272
47 Non-ferrous metal products, M	290, 296, 297, 309, 310, 312-314 316-330, 333
48 Iron and steel products, M	259, 264, 266, 268, 269, 273, 374, 276, 278, 298, 300, 302-307, 334-338, 341-349
49 Machinery and equipment, M	350-366, 383-385, 387
50 Aircraft, including parts, M	368-371
51 Autos, trucks, and parts, M	372, 373, 375-377, 379-381
52 Buses and locomotives, M	374, 378, 382
53 Transportation equipment, M	386, 388-390
54 Electrical products, M	391-395, 397-399, 401-409, 412-414
55 Mineral products, M	417, 422-433, 435
56 Petroleum Products, M	436-445, 601
57 Pharmaceuticals, M	455, 460-462
58 Chemical, M	451, 452, 454, 456-459, 463, 464, 471 472, 474, 478, 479, 482, 494, 497, 499-502, 506, 508, 510-513, 517-522, 540, 541, 548
59 Industrial chemicals, M	524, 526-539, 542-547, 549-551
60 Scientific equipment, M	553-557
61 Jewellery, M	558-561
62 Plastic products, M	564-567
63 End products, M	562, 563, 568-570, 572, 576-580, 573-575, 581
64 Raw cotton, NCM	639
65 Rubber, NCM	640
66 Cane sugar, NCM	641
67 Cocoa beans, NCM	642
68 Green coffee, NCM	643
69 Tropical fruit, NCM	644
70 Rice and hops, NCM	007, 020
71 Live animals, R	001-004, 006
72 Wheat, R	008
73 Other grain, R	009
74 Milk, unprocessed, R	010
75 Eggs, R	011
76 Honey and beeswax, R	012
77 Nuts, fruits, berries, R	013, 014

TABLE 3.1 cont'd.

Name	644-level commodity code
78 Vegetables, R	015
79 Hay, grass, and nursery, R	016-018
80 Oil seeds, oil, nuts, R	019
81 Tobacco, R	021
82 Fur, R	005, 022, 031
83 Wool in the grease, R	023
84 Logs and bolts, R	025
85 Poles and pit props, R	026
86 Pulpwood, R	027
87 Other crude wood, R	028
88 Custom forestry, R	029
89 Fish landings, R	030
90 Metal ores, R	032
91 Radio-active ores, R	033
92 Iron ores, R	034
93 Gold and platinum ores, R	035, 036
94 Crude oil, R	038
95 Natural gas, R	039
96 Coal, R	037, 040
97 Sulphur, R	041
98 Asbestos, R	042
99 Salt and gypsum, R	043, 044
100 Abrasives and clay, R	046, 047
101 Non-metallic minerals, R	045, 048
102 Sand and gravels, R	049
103 Stone, R	050

1 Producer names with the designation D are those producing for domestic market. Those designated with E produce exported commodities. The capital letter M implies that the producer group is import competing, and NCM means non-competing imports. Resource commodities are denoted R.

alternative to Canadian production, and we wished to be assured that the US price represented a valid alternative to the Canadian price.

Because of the flexibility of the Canadian input-output table it was possible to achieve an aggregation which could best meet the criteria discussed in chapter one. The results of the preliminary empirical work can be seen in Table 3.1. The classification of each commodity group is indicated by the letter after the verbal name. A D after the verbal name indicates that the commodities in that group are domestic, an E after the verbal name indicates the commodities of that group are exported, and an M after the verbal name indicates that the group consists of commodities that must compete with imports. The R following a verbal name indicates that the group is composed of resource commodities, and the letters

NCM after a verbal name indicate that the commodities in such a case are non-competing imports. The first twenty-eight commodity classes in the table are domestic. The next nine classes are exportable goods. Commodity groups 38-63 are importable and groups 64-70 are non-competing imports. The remaining groups are resource commodities.

Because of the large number of classes defined in this project it was possible to distinguish between technically similar groups according to their differing roles in international trade. It will be noted, for example, that the verbal title 'non-ferrous metal products,' appears twice on the list in Table 3.1. Products of this type in group 14 were sold principally on the domestic market in 1961 while those in group 34 are products which are exported. In some cases it has been necessary to create three categories for a commodity group – for example, intermediate iron and steel products. In order to prevent confusion on this point we refer to each class by both its verbal name and its class number.

DIRECT COSTS OF INDUSTRIAL GROUPS

The presentation of the 1961 Canadian input-output tables differs from the usual format adopted for such data. There are two rectangular tables instead of the more conventional single square table. One rectangular table shows the amount of each commodity shipped to each industry and a second rectangular table shows the amount of each commodity produced by each industry. In this form the tables leave the user a maximum of flexibility and it is possible to derive a single square matrix (Statistics Canada, 15-501, 1969, 138). The initial data tape supplied to this project was equivalent to a 125 by 125 inter-industry table. This was then aggregated to the 103-level and finally adjusted to a per dollar of output basis. The data, in this form are displayed in Table 3.4 at the end of this chapter.

Of the 103 industrial groups, only sixty-three produce commodities other than resources. Each of the sixty-three purchases inputs from the remaining 103 as indicated in Table 3.4. Rows 1-63 in any of the columns of Table 3.4 show purchases per dollar of output from other producing groups, rows 64-70 of Table 3.4 are purchases on non-competing imports, and rows 71-103 are purchases of resource commodities. The verbal name for any column is the same as the verbal name given to the corresponding row. Column totals must add to one minus the commodity tax.

Table 3.4 is used in part two to analyse the cost relationships of various groups but it is also used in connection with Table 3.2 and 3.3. Table 3.2 shows the relative cost dependence of each industry on the domestic, export, import and resource sectors respectively. The percentage of costs spent in these sectors are shown in columns one, two, three, and four. Column five shows value added. In column six the percentage of production shipped to other industries is shown and in column seven the reader can determine commodity taxes per unit of output. The percentage change in the output necessary under free trade to reach the optimal level of production in each industry is displayed in column eight. The data of Tables 3.2 and 3.3 were also used in the discriminant analysis of chapter one.

WEIGHTED AVERAGE TARIFFS

The tariff schedules of both canada and the United States are exceedingly complicated documents. Rates are expressed in both specific and *ad valorem* terms and sometimes a mixture of rates is given. The verbal titles and other description for a tariff item are often lengthy, specifying such detail as weight, length, or other characteristics of the product imported. At an early stage we were confronted with two rather intractable problems. First of all, it was necessary to find *ad valorem* equivalents for many tariffs, and secondly, it was necessary to find an acceptable form of aggregation.

Most Canadian tariffs are specified in *ad valorem* terms. Those which are specified as specific or specific plus *ad valorem* can be converted to *ad valorem* if unit values of imports are known. Fortunately, such unit values can be inferred from Statistics Canada (65-203, 1969) data giving the value and quantity of goods imported into Canada. Tariff rates were taken from the 1965 office consolidated version of the customs tariff, and adjustments were made to put the 1965 rates back to the 1961 level. These rates were then adjusted forward to the level that would apply after the Kennedy Round.

Aggregation up to the 644-level of commodity classification proceeded by simple unweighted averaging. The process was greatly facilitated by a set of computer cards obtained from the External Trade Division.[1] These cards give the code numbers of commodities most frequently assigned to each tariff item. As noted above, the relationship between the import commodity code and the 644-level of classification is given by Statistics Canada and this greatly simplifies the task of aggregation in each of the 644-level classes. Tariffs on commodities at the 103-level of the commodity code were computed as weighted averages using the output levels of commodity groups at the 644-level of classification as weights.

Data for the United States tariff are based on the Committee for Economic Development (1963) publication. This document performs the essential task of defining the United States tariff classification in terms of the Standard International Commodity Classification. It was then possible to group the United

TABLE 3.2 PERCENTAGE OF COST SPENT IN VARIOUS SECTORS, SHIPMENTS, COMMODITY TAXES AND CHANGES IN INDUSTRIAL OUTPUTS.

NAME OF PRODUCER GROUP	(1) DOMESTIC SECTOR % RANK	(2) EXPORT SECTOR % RANK	(3) IMPORT COMPUTING SECTOR % RANK	(4) RESOURCE SECTOR % RANK	(5) VALUE ADDED % RANK	(6) SHIPMENTS OF INTERMEDIATE INTERGOODS % RANK	(7) COMMODITY TAXES % RANK	(8) CHANGE IN OUTPUT % RANK
1. SERVICES TO AGRICULTURE,D	22.10 (23)	7.77 (32)	8.23 (47)	3.51 (30)	54.70 (8)	92.20 (13)	3.69 (4)	-.04 (38)
2. SERVICES TO MINING,D	17.38 (40)	15.66 (11)	9.26 (44)	.50 (48)	56.01 (6)	55.98 (31)	1.19 (24)	-.02 (31)
3. MEAT EX. FISH + POULTRY,D	22.30 (19)	4.70 (49)	4.26 (56)	44.53 (4)	22.95 (55)	29.12 (47)	.76 (53)	-.28 (44)
4. PROCESSED POULTRY,C	25.54 (15)	4.40 (56)	2.24 (60)	36.40 (6)	31.02 (48)	22.35 (52)	.78 (51)	-.19 (43)
5. DAIRY PRODUCTS,D	15.40 (45)	3.70 (58)	3.89 (57)	54.58 (2)	20.36 (59)	20.88 (53)	1.06 (33)	-.08 (41)
6. FEED MEAL,D	23.81 (18)	16.54 (9)	15.63 (33)	30.38 (8)	14.81 (61)	95.58 (11)	-1.42 (62)	-.05 (39)
7. CEREAL AND BAKERY,C	30.50 (9)	15.43 (13)	11.71 (39)	1.90 (35)	38.93 (33)	12.52 (59)	1.53 (14)	-.02 (32)
8. SUGAR REFINERY PRODUCTS,C	4.29 (62)	4.99 (48)	46.71 (3)	10.71 (16)	28.54 (51)	55.39 (32)	.77 (52)	-1.33 (48)
9. CONFECTIONARY PRODUCTS,D	30.34 (10)	8.21 (29)	23.28 (18)	4.79 (28)	32.49 (47)	.74 (63)	.88 (44)	.01 (29)
10. PROCESSED TOBACCO,D	41.85 (4)	2.21 (60)	1.74 (62)	30.77 (7)	22.84 (56)	24.27 (51)	.59 (61)	-.01 (28)
11. LEATHER,D	55.96 (3)	7.07 (36)	10.20 (41)	.90 (41)	24.85 (54)	99.65 (3)	1.02 (36)	-9.00 (53)
12. WOOD PRODUCTS,D	17.99 (38)	17.37 (8)	17.95 (32)	5.23 (26)	40.53 (30)	44.77 (36)	.93 (42)	-.06 (22)
13. IRON AND STEEL INTERMED,C	18.84 (34)	14.73 (15)	14.33 (35)	8.73 (19)	42.41 (26)	98.03 (8)	.97 (38)	1.16 (15)
14. NONFERROUS METAL PROD,C	15.93 (47)	30.60 (1)	8.23 (46)	15.87 (13)	38.52 (52)	89.44 (14)	.78 (50)	.52 (19)
15. ELECTRICAL PRODUCTS,D	11.89 (56)	20.20 (4)	28.90 (11)	.10 (59)	39.16 (34)	35.35 (33)	.74 (55)	-.04 (16)
16. MINERAL PRODUCTS,C	26.25 (13)	15.46 (12)	5.44 (52)	8.74 (18)	42.09 (28)	98.57 (6)	2.02 (10)	-.04 (37)
17. EXPLOSIVES,C	25.75 (14)	10.54 (21)	14.89 (34)	1.05 (40)	46.91 (14)	70.79 (25)	.85 (47)	-.06 (40)
18. CHEMICALS,D	17.05 (42)	10.66 (20)	17.99 (31)	5.96 (24)	46.55 (16)	85.08 (20)	1.79 (12)	-2.18 (50)
19. DRESSING AND DYEING,D	14.26 (48)	9.38 (25)	18.66 (28)	.77 (46)	55.67 (7)	103.00 (1)	1.06 (32)	-9.16 (54)
20. CONSTRUCTION,C	26.43 (12)	7.36 (34)	23.23 (19)	1.31 (38)	38.09 (36)	15.05 (57)	3.58 (5)	-.01 (30)
21. TRANSPORTATION,D	21.87 (25)	4.66 (50)	5.23 (53)	2.29 (34)	63.89 (3)	46.65 (35)	2.05 (9)	-.32 (45)
22. ELECTRIC POWER,D	30.33 (11)	1.06 (63)	.44 (63)	.88 (43)	66.53 (2)	59.77 (27)	.76 (54)	-.04 (36)
23. WATER SERVICES,D	30.52 (8)	6.76 (38)	6.19 (50)	2.57 (33)	44.67 (21)	15.04 (58)	9.29 (2)	.16 (21)
24. COMMUNICATIONS,D	18.56 (35)	1.60 (62)	2.13 (61)	.01 (62)	81.10 (1)	57.89 (29)	-3.40 (63)	-.02 (33)
25. BUSINESS SERVICE,D	19.74 (30)	4.10 (54)	2.28 (59)	.85 (45)	60.32 (5)	31.84 (45)	12.70 (1)	-.04 (35)
26. PERSONAL SERVICE,D	21.00 (27)	7.10 (33)	7.70 (49)	.11 (56)	61.83 (4)	24.82 (50)	2.25 (7)	-.03 (34)
27. ADVERTISING AND TRAVEL,D	70.39 (1)	4.11 (53)	12.51 (37)	.01 (63)	9.14 (62)	99.88 (2)	3.85 (3)	-.32 (46)
28. PAPER PRODUCTS,D	32.09 (7)	10.54 (22)	8.54 (45)	9.66 (17)	37.78 (39)	83.18 (15)	1.39 (18)	-.05 (23)
29. FISH PRODUCTS,E	12.74 (54)	11.29 (19)	4.72 (54)	49.34 (3)	21.28 (57)	40.10 (38)	.63 (58)	.03 (24)
30. FLOUR, MALT AND STARCH, E	20.57 (23)	14.07 (16)	10.66 (40)	27.41 (10)	26.14 (53)	39.62 (39)	1.16 (26)	.54 (18)
31. BEET, PULP AND SUGAR,E	22.12 (22)	8.06 (30)	23.61 (20)	6.73 (20)	37.80 (38)	52.36 (34)	2.08 (8)	-10.00 (57)
32. WOOD, PULP AND PAPER,F	10.87 (57)	14.00 (17)	3.86 (58)	27.89 (9)				

33. IRON AND STEEL INTERMED,E	9.99 (59)	18.51 (5)	8.04 (48)	19.82 (12)	42.71 (25)	98.56 (7)	.95 (40)	10.00 (1)
34. NONFERROUS METAL PROD,E	6.66 (63)	26.60 (2)	4.33 (55)	42.19 (5)	19.39 (60)	99.30 (4)	.83 (48)	.02 (26)
35. INORGANIC CHEMICALS,E	16.46 (44)	22.35 (3)	12.64 (36)	6.49 (22)	40.36 (31)	95.07 (12)	1.70 (13)	5.53 (14)
36. LIQUOR AND BEER,E	22.70 (20)	15.22 (14)	9.91 (43)	3.32 (31)	46.56 (15)	8.74 (60)	2.29 (6)	10.00 (2)
37. REPAIR AND SUPPLY,E	67.68 (2)	1.72 (61)	28.50 (12)	.30 (50)	.00 (63)	85.97 (19)	1.80 (11)	-1.25 (47)
38. PROCESSED FOODS,M	23.92 (16)	6.26 (44)	23.67 (17)	15.47 (14)	29.64 (50)	32.88 (43)	1.05 (34)	-5.65 (52)
39. ALCOHOL AND WINE,M	17.27 (41)	6.87 (37)	18.16 (30)	13.56 (15)	42.74 (24)	18.07 (56)	1.39 (19)	10.00 (3)
40. RUBBER PRODUCTS,M	12.14 (55)	5.25 (47)	38.07 (6)	.69 (47)	42.79 (23)	65.43 (26)	1.06 (31)	10.00 (4)
41. LEATHER PRODUCTS,M	35.78 (5)	4.03 (55)	19.99 (25)	.08 (59)	39.48 (32)	7.88 (61)	.63 (59)	-10.00 (58)
42. COTTON TEXTILE PRODUCTS,M	9.49 (60)	4.44 (51)	50.69 (1)	.43 (49)	34.08 (46)	87.22 (17)	.88 (46)	-10.00 (59)
43. WOOL TEXTILE PRODUCTS,M	8.72 (61)	6.56 (40)	41.53 (5)	5.04 (27)	37.33 (41)	81.88 (23)	.82 (49)	.61 (17)
44. OTHER TEXTILE PRODUCTS,M	13.53 (52)	3.91 (57)	42.88 (4)	1.68 (37)	37.32 (42)	32.65 (44)	.68 (57)	-9.39 (55)
45. PRINTING,M	19.10 (33)	15.89 (10)	10.14 (42)	.04 (61)	53.64 (9)	57.31 (30)	1.18 (25)	10.00 (5)
46. GRAPHITE AND CARBON,M	10.33 (58)	17.54 (6)	11.73 (38)	21.34 (11)	38.13 (35)	99.17 (5)	.93 (41)	-10.00 (60)
47. NONFERROUS METAL PROD,M	23.88 (17)	17.43 (7)	19.78 (26)	.23 (53)	37.81 (37)	87.53 (16)	.88 (45)	10.00 (6)
48. IRON AND STEEL PRODUCTS,M	19.98 (29)	11.74 (18)	20.66 (24)	5.50 (25)	41.00 (29)	96.39 (9)	1.11 (29)	-3.76 (51)
49. MACHINERY AND EQUIPMENT,M	21.47 (26)	6.35 (42)	24.79 (15)	1.13 (39)	46.97 (19)	39.40 (40)	1.29 (20)	-10.00 (56)
50. AIRCRAFT INC. PARTS,M	13.89 (49)	6.34 (43)	32.06 (9)	.07 (60)	46.18 (17)	20.48 (54)	1.45 (15)	10.00 (7)
51. AUTOS, TRUCKS AND PARTS,M	13.61 (51)	5.27 (46)	49.60 (2)	.23 (52)	30.17 (49)	33.95 (42)	1.12 (28)	10.00 (13)
52. BUSES AND LOCOMOTIVES,M	19.22 (32)	7.45 (33)	37.37 (7)	.19 (55)	34.58 (45)	25.04 (49)	1.20 (23)	10.00 (8)
53. TRANSPORATION EQUIPMENT,M	13.79 (50)	4.22 (52)	27.52 (13)	.11 (57)	53.28 (10)	6.19 (62)	1.08 (30)	10.00 (9)
54. ELECTRICAL PRODUCTS,M	19.31 (31)	6.50 (41)	29.38 (10)	.21 (54)	43.55 (22)	42.96 (37)	1.02 (37)	10.00 (10)
55. MINERAL PRODUCTS,M	16.03 (46)	10.46 (23)	18.73 (29)	6.19 (23)	47.16 (12)	82.18 (22)	1.43 (16)	-.09 (42)
56. PETROLEUM PRODUCTS,M	13.03 (53)	2.32 (59)	5.71 (51)	56.87 (1)	21.04 (58)	53.71 (28)	.60 (60)	.01 (27)
57. PHARMACEUTICALS,M	32.53 (6)	6.70 (39)	22.04 (22)	.88 (42)	36.71 (44)	28.95 (48)	1.12 (27)	-10.00 (61)
58. CHEMICALS,M	22.43 (21)	8.05 (31)	26.60 (14)	4.22 (29)	37.47 (40)	83.04 (21)	1.22 (22)	-2.06 (49)
59. INDUSTRIAL CHEMICALS,M	16.87 (43)	9.19 (26)	24.38 (16)	3.16 (32)	44.98 (18)	86.92 (18)	1.41 (17)	-10.00 (62)
60. SCIENTIFIC EQUIPMENT,M	17.68 (39)	9.07 (27)	23.12 (21)	.27 (51)	48.94 (11)	29.59 (46)	.92 (43)	-10.00 (11)
61. JEWELRY,M	18.30 (37)	8.45 (28)	16.96 (27)	6.62 (21)	46.97 (13)	18.90 (55)	.70 (56)	.37 (20)
62. PLASTIC PRODUCTS,M	18.37 (36)	6.07 (45)	35.88 (8)	1.77 (36)	36.88 (43)	77.90 (24)	1.03 (35)	10.00 (12)
63. END PRODUCTS,M	22.01 (24)	9.53 (24)	21.77 (23)	.88 (44)	44.84 (20)	38.44 (41)	.96 (39)	-10.00 (63)

States tariff according to the Canadian 644-level input-output classification. As in the case of the Canadian tariff, rates up to the 644-level were obtained as simple unweighted averages. To obtain rates at the 103-level, weighted averages were used with the outputs of commodities at the 644-level of classification serving as weights.

Both Canada and the United States make some use of quotas (including voluntary quotas) for the purpose of protecting domestic industry. With some exceptions, this means of protecting domestic industry has been almost exclusively applied to resource commodities. The simulation is designed to study the interaction between the Canadian tariff and the Canadian resource endowment. The 1961 resource absorption rates are taken to represent the Canadian endowment and are therefore assumed to be fixed. It is implicit that 1961 resource trade levels are also fixed at the 1961 level. Insofar as either the US or Canadian quotas affect resource trade, this aspect of the problem is already incorporated in the model. In practice, of course, Canada, like all nations, will modify its resource base through direct exports, but it is assumed that the residual left for absorption through commodity production is relatively stable from year to year. (The rationale for this was discussed in chapter one).

Certain other features of the Canadian tariff proved so difficult that an arbitrary decision concerning them had to be made. There are some tariff items (on fruits and vegetables) which vary over the growing season. In such cases, it was assumed that the lower of the two possible rates were applied. Schedule B of the Canadian tariff schedule presents a different type of problem. There are a number of commodities listed in schedule B which are subject to drawback (usually of 99 per cent). Typically the drawback applies to imports used as intermediate goods under specially prescribed circumstances. Because these goods are defined so narrowly, they lose their identity in the broadly defined commodity classes considered in this study. There is little doubt that drawbacks have a substantial effect on the cost of producing particular goods. Their effect on any broad category of production, on the other hand is more doubtful. It has not been possible to deal with these systematically and we must, therefore, leave it to the reader to make allowances in the cases of particular commodities.

Data showing the weighted average Canadian and US tariffs and the level of antiprotection are displayed in Table 3.3. The second column of Table 3.3 is the weighted average US tariff computed with Canadian output levels serving as weights. The Canadian pre-Kennedy tariff is shown in column 3 of Table 3.3 and the pre-Kennedy antiprotection of the Canadian-U.S. tariff is shown in column 5. Column 4 is the post-Kennedy weighted average Canadian tariff and column 6 is the level of antiprotection after the Kennedy Round. Rankings are shown in parenthesis.

CONSTRUCTION OF THE LINEAR PROGRAMMING FORMAT

The construction of the linear programming model from the coefficients displayed in Table 3.4 is most easily visualized with reference to the example displayed in Table 2.2. In the example, the problem was concerned with finding the optimum output levels of eight producing industries. In the applied model there are sixty-three such industrial groups. Corresponding to the first eight columns of Table 2.2, there are sixty-three columns in the model. The coefficients in the sixty-three columns are the same as the coefficients in the sixty-three columns shown in Table 3.4 except for the major diagonal.[2] If we subtract one from each of these, such coefficients could also be used in the linear programming format. They would then each be negative and appear as illustrated in Table 2.2.

The export and import columns appearing in the example Table 2.2 do not appear in Table 3.4. In the linear programming format these coefficients are all zeroes or ones except for the entries that appear in the 106th row. The tariff rates needed to make up this row are displayed in Table 3.3. Similarly, the objective function for the simulation is made up of the commodity tax rates shown in Table 3.2 and the Canadian tariff rates shown in Table 3.3. The final model has 106 rows and 296 columns. There are 63 columns of production activities, 63 columns of export activities, 63 columns of import activities, 106 slack variables, and the retailing activity. This last column of coefficients is obtained by dividing consumption of each commodity in 1961 by total household expenditure for 1961.

The linear programming format determines the optimal levels of output in each industrial group. This optimization is subject to the condition that the amount of each resource absorbed cannot exceed the amount actually available in 1961. The output levels of resource commodities act as right-hand-side constants. The economy is not allowed to use any more of any resource than it had available in 1961 and it is required to produce at least as much of all non-resource commodities as is required (1) to supply the intermediate goods needed in the production of resource goods, (2) to supply the requirements of government, and (3) to supply the actual amounts of investment goods produced in 1961. As noted in chapter one, no industry is allowed to reduce its output below ninety per cent of the 1961 level and none is allowed to increase its output by more than ten per cent. To establish these boundaries, two constraints must be added for each industry. It is also assumed that there is no reversal in the direction of trade. Commodities exported in 1961 are constrained to be exported or domestic in the free trade format, goods imported in 1961 are

TABLE 3.3 TRANSPORT COST AND TARIFF DATA FOR SIXTY-THREE PRODUCER GROUPS.

NAME OF PRODUCER GROUP	TRANSPORT COST AMOUNT	RANK	PRE-KENNEDY U.S. TARIFF AMOUNT	RANK	PRE-KENNEDY CANADIAN TARIFF AMOUNT	RANK	POST-KENNEDY CANADIAN TARIFF AMOUNT	RANK	PRE-KENNEDY ANTI-PROTECTION AMOUNT	RANK	POST-KENNEDY ANTI-PROTECTION AMOUNT	RANK
1. SERVICES TO AGRICULTURE,D	.044	(11)	.000	(51)	.000	(52)	.000	(52)	-.010	(43)	-.008	(45)
2. SERVICES TO MINING,D	.064	(7)	.000	(52)	.000	(53)	.000	(53)	-.009	(46)	-.008	(43)
3. MEAT EX. FISH + POULTRY,D	.025	(41)	.073	(34)	.105	(39)	.088	(34)	-.005	(53)	-.005	(53)
4. PROCESSED POULTRY,D	.030	(25)	.000	(53)	.121	(35)	.121	(21)	-.003	(58)	-.002	(60)
5. DAIRY PRODUCTS,D	.013	(59)	.081	(28)	.148	(19)	.145	(11)	-.005	(52)	-.004	(55)
6. FEED MEAL,D	.051	(9)	.049	(43)	.111	(36)	.068	(45)	-.016	(33)	-.019	(28)
7. CEREAL AND BAKERY,D	.034	(19)	.031	(48)	.143	(22)	.114	(25)	-.007	(47)	-.010	(35)
8. SUGAR REFINERY PRODUCTS,D	.029	(27)	.121	(17)	.185	(11)	.182	(6)	-.031	(15)	-.008	(44)
9. CONFECTIONARY PRODUCTS,D	.031	(23)	.109	(22)	.203	(9)	.169	(7)	-.025	(20)	-.024	(18)
10. PROCESSED TOBACCO,D	.017	(58)	.386	(1)	.494	(1)	.262	(1)	-.003	(56)	-.002	(59)
11. LEATHER,D	.111	(3)	.075	(33)	.153	(17)	.134	(16)	-.011	(38)	-.009	(41)
12. WOOD PRODUCTS,D	.051	(10)	.116	(19)	.204	(8)	.160	(9)	-.024	(23)	-.022	(22)
13. IRON AND STEEL INTERMED,D	.028	(36)	.055	(41)	.094	(42)	.084	(37)	-.014	(35)	-.013	(34)
14. NONFERROUS METAL PROD,D	.321	(53)	.081	(29)	.131	(28)	.080	(40)	-.001	(60)	-.005	(54)
15. ELECTRICAL PRODUCTS,D	.023	(45)	.140	(11)	.136	(25)	.099	(30)	-.034	(12)	-.033	(11)
16. MINERAL PRODUCTS,D	.036	(17)	.117	(18)	.126	(31)	.075	(43)	-.009	(45)	-.007	(47)
17. EXPLOSIVES ,D	.023	(44)	.188	(5)	.099	(40)	.095	(31)	-.016	(34)	-.014	(33)
18. CHEMICALS,D	.032	(21)	.146	(9)	.084	(45)	.083	(38)	-.021	(27)	-.017	(30)
19. DRESSING AND DYEING,D	.024	(43)	.000	(54)	.000	(54)	.000	(54)	-.023	(25)	-.019	(27)
20. CONSTRUCTION,D	.073	(5)	.000	(55)	.000	(55)	.000	(55)	-.026	(19)	-.024	(19)
21. TRANSPORTATION,D	.057	(8)	.000	(56)	.000	(56)	.000	(56)	-.007	(48)	-.006	(50)
22. ELECTRIC POWER,D	.009	(63)	.000	(57)	.000	(57)	.000	(57)	-.001	(62)	-.000	(62)
23. WATER SERVICES,D	.043	(13)	.000	(58)	.000	(58)	.000	(58)	-.009	(44)	-.006	(48)
24. COMMUNICATIONS,D	.065	(6)	.000	(59)	.000	(59)	.000	(59)	-.003	(59)	-.002	(61)
25. BUSINESS SERVICE,D	.010	(62)	.000	(60)	.000	(60)	.000	(60)	-.003	(57)	-.003	(58)
26. PERSONAL SERVICE,D	.025	(56)	.000	(61)	.000	(61)	.000	(61)	-.016	(41)	-.009	(42)
27. ADVERTISING AND TRAVEL,D	.129	(2)	.000	(62)	.000	(62)	.000	(62)	-.014	(36)	-.010	(37)
28. PAPER PRODUCTS,D	.023	(50)	.098	(24)	.162	(14)	.140	(14)	-.011	(37)	-.009	(38)
29. FISH PRODUCTS,E	.323	(46)	.069	(37)	.089	(44)	.048	(48)	-.004	(55)	-.006	(51)
30. FLOUR, MALT AND STARCH, E	.047	(12)	.070	(36)	.173	(12)	.109	(27)	-.007	(49)	-.009	(39)
31. BEET, PULP AND SUGAR,E	.037	(16)	.076	(31)	.239	(6)	.153	(10)	-.019	(31)	-.016	(31)
32. WOOD, PULP AND PAPER, E	.024	(42)	.022	(50)	.076	(46)	.049	(47)	-.004	(54)	-.004	(57)

33. IRON AND STEEL INTERMED,E	.027 (37)	.031 (49)	.026 (51)	.026 (51)	-.006 (51)	-.006 (49)
34. NONFERROUS METAL PROD,E	.012 (60)	.036 (47)	.057 (48)	.044 (49)	.003 (63)	-.000 (63)
35. INORGANIC CHEMICALS,E	.028 (34)	.043 (44)	.046 (50)	.041 (50)	-.010 (42)	-.009 (40)
36. LIQUOR AND BEER,E	.021 (54)	.146 (9)	.441 (2)	.073 (44)	-.061 (61)	-.004 (56)
37. REPAIR AND SUPPLY,F	.615 (1)	.000 (63)	.000 (63)	.000 (63)	-.033 (14)	-.029 (13)
38. PROCESSED FOODS,W	.129 (28)	.091 (26)	.136 (26)	.091 (33)	-.040 (8)	-.036 (7)
39. ALCOHOL AND WINE,M	.038 (15)	.124 (15)	.134 (27)	.138 (15)	-.021 (29)	-.017 (29)
40. RUBBER PRODUCTS,M	.023 (49)	.096 (25)	.148 (18)	.125 (18)	-.052 (5)	-.047 (5)
41. LEATHER PRODUCTS,M	.031 (24)	.115 (21)	.247 (5)	.224 (3)	-.046 (9)	-.035 (8)
42. COTTON TEXTILE PRODUCTS,M	.020 (55)	.131 (14)	.217 (7)	.192 (5)	-.070 (3)	-.058 (3)
43. WOOL TEXTILE PRODUCTS,M	.027 (38)	.330 (2)	.247 (4)	.210 (4)	-.084 (1)	-.073 (1)
44. OTHER TEXTILE PRODUCTS,M	.036 (18)	.228 (3)	.255 (3)	.225 (2)	-.073 (2)	-.065 (2)
45. PRINTING,M	.011 (61)	.081 (27)	.122 (33)	.113 (26)	-.011 (40)	-.008 (46)
46. GRAPHITE AND CARBON,M	.025 (39)	.076 (30)	.130 (29)	.079 (41)	-.011 (39)	-.010 (36)
47. NONFERROUS METAL PROD,M	.023 (47)	.067 (38)	.161 (15)	.123 (20)	-.020 (30)	-.019 (26)
48. IRON AND STEEL PRODUCTS,M	.028 (33)	.043 (45)	.143 (21)	.124 (19)	-.022 (26)	-.021 (25)
49. MACHINERY AND EQUIPMENT,M	.028 (30)	.064 (40)	.110 (37)	.101 (28)	-.024 (24)	-.025 (17)
50. AIRCRAFT INC. PARTS,M	.019 (57)	.104 (23)	.051 (49)	.078 (42)	-.035 (11)	-.031 (12)
51. AUTOS, TRUCKS AND PARTS,M	.032 (20)	.052 (42)	.098 (41)	.081 (39)	-.066 (4)	-.051 (4)
52. BUSES AND LOCOMOTIVES,M	.039 (14)	.124 (16)	.128 (30)	.091 (32)	-.048 (6)	-.040 (6)
53. TRANSPORTATION EQUIPMENT,M	.028 (32)	.039 (46)	.147 (20)	.120 (22)	-.029 (16)	-.028 (14)
54. ELECTRICAL PRODUCTS,M	.025 (40)	.135 (13)	.169 (13)	.144 (12)	-.037 (10)	-.034 (9)
55. MINERAL PRODUCTS,M	.028 (31)	.144 (10)	.137 (24)	.126 (17)	-.018 (32)	-.016 (32)
56. PETROLEUM PRODUCTS,M	.085 (4)	.076 (32)	.067 (47)	.364 (46)	-.006 (50)	-.005 (52)
57. PHARMACEUTICALS,M	.028 (35)	.072 (35)	.159 (15)	.099 (29)	-.024 (22)	-.023 (20)
58. CHEMICALS,M	.030 (26)	.115 (20)	.125 (32)	.114 (24)	-.034 (13)	-.023 (15)
59. INDUSTRIAL CHEMICALS,M	.032 (22)	.064 (39)	.109 (38)	.086 (35)	-.028 (17)	-.023 (21)
60. SCIENTIFIC EQUIPMENT,M	.022 (51)	.211 (4)	.091 (43)	.086 (36)	-.027 (18)	-.025 (16)
61. JEWELRY,M	.021 (52)	.158 (7)	.142 (23)	.120 (23)	-.021 (28)	-.021 (24)
62. PLASTIC PRODUCTS,M	.023 (48)	.172 (6)	.122 (34)	.141 (13)	-.042 (7)	-.034 (10)
63. END PRODUCTS,M	.029 (29)	.116 (12)	.197 (10)	.163 (9)	-.025 (21)	-.022 (23)

TABLE 3.4   SHIPMENTS PER DOLLAR OF OUTPUT

SHIPPING GROUP

RECEIVING GROUP

	(1)	(2)	(3)	(4)	(5)	(6)	(7)	(8)	(9)	(10)	(11)	(12)	(13)

TABLE 3.4 SHIPMENTS PER DOLLAR OF OUTPUT (CONTINUED)

RECEIVING GROUP

SHIPPING GROUP

COCOA BEANS, NCM
COFFEE, NCM
TEA, NCM
OIL PROPS, S
HIDES AND SKINS, S
UNPROCESSED MILK, R
EGGS, R
HONEY, BEESWAX, R
FRUITS, AND BERRIES, R
VEGETABLES, AND NURSERY, R
RAW FURS, AND NUTS, R
WOOL, GREASE, R
PULP, BOLT PROPS, F
OTHER FOREST PRODUCTS, R
CUSTOM FEEDING, R
IRON ORES, R
IRON ORES, PLATINUM ORES, R
GOLD ORES, R
CRUDE PETROLEUM, R
COAL GAS, R
ASBESTOS, R
SALT, GYPSUM, R
ABRASIVES AND CLAY, R
SAND AND GRAVEL, R
STONE, R
OTHER MINERALS, R
VALUE ADDED
BALANCE OF TRADE

TABLE 3.4 SHIPMENTS PER DOLLAR OF OUTPUT (CONTINUED)

SHIPPING GROUP   RECEIVING GROUP

		(27)	(28)	(29)	(30)	(31)	(32)	(33)	(34)	(35)	(36)	(37)	(38)	(39)
1.	SERVICES TO AGRICULTURE,D	.000	.000	.000	.000	.009	.000	.000	.000	.000	.000	.000	.000	.000
2.	SERVICES TO MINING,D	.000	.000	.000	.020	.000	.000	.000	.000	.000	.002	.005	.015	.002
3.	MEAT EX. FISH + POULTRY,D	.000	.000	.015	.020	.009	.000	.000	.000	.002	.002	.005	.015	.002
4.	PROCESSED POULTRY,D	.000	.000	.000	.001	.001	.000	.000	.000	.000	.000	.001	.007	.000
5.	DAIRY PRODUCTS,D	.000	.000	.000	.007	.004	.000	.000	.000	.000	.000	.003	.009	.000
6.	FEED MEAL,D	.000	.000	.000	.002	.037	.000	.000	.000	.000	.000	.000	.000	.000
7.	CEREAL AND BAKERY,D	.000	.000	.000	.000	.000	.000	.000	.000	.000	.000	.002	.000	.000
8.	SUGAR REFINERY PRODUCTS,D	.000	.000	.000	.015	.009	.000	.000	.000	.000	.000	.000	.034	.009
9.	CONFECTIONARY PRODUCTS,D	.000	.000	.000	.001	.000	.000	.000	.000	.000	.000	.000	.000	.000
10.	PROCESSED TOBACCO,D	.000	.000	.000	.000	.000	.000	.000	.000	.000	.000	.000	.000	.000
11.	LEATHER,D	.000	.000	.000	.000	.000	.000	.000	.000	.000	.000	.000	.000	.000
12.	WOOD PRODUCTS,D	.000	.005	.007	.000	.001	.008	.002	.000	.007	.006	.000	.000	.004
13.	IRON AND STEEL INTERMED,D	.000	.001	.006	.000	.000	.005	.020	.000	.007	.001	.000	.000	.000
14.	NONFERROUS METAL PROD,D	.000	.003	.000	.000	.001	.005	.006	.007	.000	.000	.004	.000	.000
15.	ELECTRICAL PRODUCTS,D	.000	.000	.000	.000	.000	.000	.007	.000	.000	.000	.002	.000	.000
16.	MINERAL PRODUCTS,D	.000	.000	.000	.000	.000	.000	.000	.000	.000	.000	.003	.000	.000
17.	EXPLOSIVES,D	.000	.000	.000	.000	.000	.000	.000	.000	.001	.001	.000	.002	.000
18.	CHEMICALS,D	.001	.000	.000	.000	.001	.000	.000	.001	.025	.000	.004	.000	.000
19.	DRESSING AND DYEING,D	.000	.000	.000	.000	.000	.000	.000	.000	.012	.000	.000	.000	.000
20.	CONSTRUCTION,D	.009	.024	.006	.002	.010	.005	.005	.007	.012	.004	.000	.003	.003
21.	TRANSPORTATION,D	.129	.023	.023	.043	.037	.024	.027	.012	.028	.021	.015	.029	.038
22.	ELECTRIC POWER,D	.001	.017	.005	.005	.005	.026	.018	.015	.032	.004	.000	.004	.002
23.	WATER SERVICES,D	.000	.001	.000	.000	.000	.001	.000	.000	.002	.002	.000	.001	.001
24.	COMMUNICATIONS,D	.064	.006	.005	.003	.003	.002	.001	.001	.005	.003	.000	.004	.002
25.	BUSINESS SERVICE,D	.300	.020	.018	.023	.023	.014	.009	.010	.019	.039	.009	.003	.013
26.	PERSONAL SERVICE,D	.016	.003	.002	.002	.002	.003	.002	.001	.004	.003	.025	.003	.002
27.	ADVERTISING AND TRAVEL,D	.180	.015	.022	.032	.038	.006	.005	.003	.014	.099	.000	.069	.070
28.	PAPER PRODUCTS,D	.012	.223	.018	.047	.031	.013	.002	.001	.020	.042	.013	.041	.026
29.	FISH PRODUCTS,D	.000	.000	.043	.001	.001	.000	.000	.000	.000	.000	.000	.001	.000
30.	FLOUR, MALT AND STARCH,E	.000	.000	.001	.075	.013	.000	.000	.000	.000	.059	.001	.008	.002
31.	BEET PULP AND SUGAR,E	.000	.000	.000	.001	.003	.000	.000	.000	.000	.000	.000	.003	.000
32.	PAPER PRODUCTS,E	.022	.036	.000	.000	.000	.059	.000	.000	.000	.000	.000	.000	.000
33.	IRON AND STEEL INTERMED,E	.000	.000	.000	.000	.000	.000	.017	.000	.000	.000	.000	.000	.000
34.	NON FERROUS METAL PROD,E	.001	.000	.000	.000	.000	.000	.067	.239	.011	.000	.000	.000	.000
35.	INORGANIC CHEMICALS,E	.000	.004	.000	.000	.010	.006	.003	.001	.134	.001	.003	.002	.000
36.	LIQUOR AND BEER,E	.008	.010	.000	.001	.000	.000	.000	.000	.000	.039	.000	.001	.029
37.	REPAIR AND SUPPLY,E	.011	.064	.068	.063	.054	.074	.099	.026	.079	.053	.012	.049	.038
38.	PROCESSED FOODS,M	.000	.001	.002	.054	.058	.002	.001	.000	.006	.008	.004	.088	.011
39.	ALCOHOL AND WINE,M	.001	.000	.000	.000	.000	.000	.000	.000	.000	.001	.000	.000	.040
40.	RUBBER PRODUCTS,M	.004	.000	.000	.000	.001	.000	.000	.000	.000	.000	.022	.000	.000
41.	LEATHER PRODUCTS,M	.002	.000	.000	.000	.000	.000	.000	.000	.000	.000	.000	.000	.000
42.	COTTON TEXTILE PRODUCTS,M	.000	.003	.000	.000	.000	.000	.000	.000	.000	.000	.000	.000	.000
43.	WOOL TEXTILE PRODUCTS,M	.000	.003	.000	.000	.000	.005	.000	.000	.000	.000	.004	.002	.000
44.	OTHER TEXTILE PRODUCTS,M	.001	.003	.001	.012	.003	.000	.000	.000	.001	.000	.004	.002	.000
45.	PRINTING,M	.078	.007	.007	.006	.006	.000	.000	.000	.000	.012	.052	.001	.014
46.	GRAPHITE AND CARBON,M	.000	.002	.000	.000	.000	.000	.004	.010	.000	.000	.001	.099	.000
47.	NONFERROUS METAL PROD,M	.000	.007	.031	.002	.008	.001	.001	.004	.004	.026	.029	.062	.000
48.	IRON AND STEEL PRODUCTS,M	.000	.001	.000	.000	.000	.000	.026	.006	.000	.000	.003	.000	.000
49.	MACHINERY AND EQUIPMENT,M	.000	.000	.000	.000	.006	.000	.008	.002	.000	.000	.072	.000	.000
50.	AIRCRAFT INC. PARTS,M	.000	.000	.000	.000	.000	.000	.000	.000	.000	.000	.021	.000	.000
51.	AUTOS, TRUCKS AND PARTS,M	.004	.000	.000	.000	.000	.000	.000	.000	.000	.000	.001	.000	.000
52.	BUSES AND LOCOMOTIVES,M	.000	.000	.000	.000	.000	.000	.000	.000	.000	.000	.000	.000	.000
53.	TRANSPORTATION EQUIPMENT,M	.001	.000	.000	.000	.000	.000	.000	.000	.000	.000	.018	.000	.000
54.	ELECTRICAL PRODUCTS,M	.001	.000	.000	.000	.000	.000	.000	.000	.000	.002	.037	.014	.076
55.	MINERAL PRODUCTS,M	.001	.003	.001	.001	.005	.001	.019	.004	.011	.051	.001	.004	.003
56.	PETROLEUM PRODUCTS,M	.016	.011	.007	.008	.025	.010	.048	.011	.011	.001	.012	.001	.000
57.	PHARMACEUTICALS,M	.000	.000	.000	.002	.011	.000	.000	.000	.002	.002	.000	.000	.000
58.	CHEMICALS,M	.003	.023	.004	.016	.018	.013	.002	.004	.044	.001	.015	.016	.000
59.	INDUSTRIAL CHEMICALS,M	.000	.009	.001	.000	.005	.004	.001	.001	.012	.003	.006	.003	.002
60.	SCIENTIFIC EQUIPMENT,M	.000	.000	.000	.000	.000	.000	.000	.000	.000	.000	.006	.000	.000
61.	JEWELRY,M	.000	.000	.000	.000	.000	.000	.000	.000	.000	.000	.000	.000	.000
62.	PLASTIC PRODUCTS,M	.001	.011	.000	.000	.001	.000	.000	.000	.000	.000	.000	.000	.000

TABLE 3.4 SHIPMENTS PER DOLLAR OF OUTPUT (CONTINUED)

SHIPPING GROUP

RECEIVING GROUP

	(40)	(41)	(42)	(43)	(44)	(45)	(46)	(47)	(48)	(49)	(50)	(51)	(52)

BEANS,NCM
COFFEE,NCM
COCOA,NCM
TEA,MATE,NCM
RAW SUGAR,M
PROCESSED MILK,+R
...BERRIES,P
NUTS AND NURSERY,+R
...NUTS,P
TOBACCO,P
...THE GREASE,R
FRUIT PROPS,+P
...WOOD,P
POTATO FOENGS,+R
CRUDE ORES,R
GOLD ORES,R
...PLATINUM ORES,R
CRUDE OIL,GAS,R
ASBESTOS,R
...GYPSUM,+R
ABRASIVES AND CLAY,R
NON-METALLIC MINERALS,P
STONE AND GRAVEL,+R
ROOFS,P
OTHER VALUE ADDED
BALANCE OF TRADE

TABLE 3.4 SHIPMENTS PER DOLLAR OF OUTPUT (CONTINUED)

SHIPPING GROUP

RECEIVING GROUP

	(53)	(54)	(55)	(56)	(57)	(58)	(59)	(60)	(61)	(62)	(63)

TABLE 3.5   RESOURCE REQUIREMENTS PER DOLLAR OF OUTPUT

PRODUCER GROUP*

RESOURCE	(1)	(2)	(3)	(4)	(5)	(6)	(7)	(8)	(9)	(10)	(11)	(12)	(13)
64. RAW COTTON*NCM	.001	.000	.001	.000	.000	.001	.001	.000	.001	.000	.001	.006	.000
65. RUBBER*NCM	.001	.000	.000	.000	.000	.006	.001	.441	.027	.001	.000	.001	.000
66. CANE SUGAR*NCM	.001	.000	.000	.000	.002	.006	.017	.000	.045	.000	.002	.001	.000
67. COCOA BEANS*NCM	.001	.000	.004	.001	.001	.007	.007	.002	.032	.001	.002	.000	.000
68. GREEN COFFEE*NCM	.000	.000	.000	.000	.000	.000	.000	.000	.000	.000	.000	.000	.000
69. TROPICAL FRUIT*NCM	.000	.000	.000	.419	.004	.041	.026	.002	.003	.006	.212	.005	.004
70. RICE AND HOPS*NCV	.021	.006	.504	.001	.000	.041	.026	.002	.009	.006	.001	.005	.004
71. LIVE ANIMALS*R	.017	.000	.002	.001	.000	.122	.034	.000	.004	.000	.002	.005	.004
72. WHEAT*R	.024	.000	.004	.001	.000	.206	.011	.000	.018	.000	.001	.000	.000
73. OTHER GRAIN*R	.002	.001	.004	.001	.001	.005	.008	.000	.017	.001	.002	.001	.000
74. UNPROCESSED MILK*R	.000	.000	.000	.001	.579	.001	.002	.000	.000	.001	.001	.001	.001
75. EGGS*R	.000	.000	.000	.000	.000	.002	.000	.000	.000	.000	.000	.000	.000
76. HONEY AND BEESWAX*R	.001	.000	.001	.001	.000	.000	.001	.000	.009	.001	.001	.000	.000
77. NUTS, FRUITS, BERRIES*R	.001	.000	.003	.001	.001	.003	.003	.000	.000	.001	.001	.000	.001
78. VEGETABLES*R	.004	.001	.000	.000	.000	.008	.008	.000	.014	.000	.002	.000	.000
79. HAY, GRASS AND NURSERY*R	.001	.000	.002	.000	.000	.004	.006	.004	.000	.000	.002	.000	.002
80. OIL SEEDS AND NUTS*R	.000	.000	.001	.000	.001	.009	.006	.000	.030	.000	.002	.001	.000
81. RAW TOBACCO*R	.000	.000	.000	.001	.000	.000	.000	.000	.000	.397	.000	.000	.000
82. FUR*R	.000	.000	.000	.000	.000	.000	.000	.000	.000	.000	.000	.001	.000
83. WOOL IN THE GREASE*R	.000	.000	.000	.000	.001	.000	.000	.000	.002	.000	.000	.001	.036
84. LOGS AND BOLTS*R	.001	.001	.002	.001	.000	.001	.002	.000	.002	.002	.001	.065	.004
85. POLES AND PIT PROPS*R	.000	.021	.000	.000	.000	.001	.000	.000	.000	.000	.001	.006	.065
86. PULPWOOD*R	.003	.007	.003	.004	.004	.004	.013	.004	.012	.013	.003	.021	.013
87. OTHER CRUDE WOOD*R	.002	.000	.000	.000	.000	.000	.000	.000	.000	.000	.003	.000	.002
88. CUSTOM FORESTRY*R	.001	.000	.000	.000	.000	.000	.000	.000	.000	.000	.003	.000	.037
89. FISH LANDINGS*R	.003	.004	.002	.001	.002	.010	.003	.000	.003	.002	.003	.008	.000
90. METAL ORES*R	.001	.000	.000	.000	.002	.004	.003	.001	.001	.000	.001	.001	.036
91. RADIO-ACTIVE ORES*R	.000	.002	.000	.000	.000	.001	.001	.000	.001	.000	.001	.003	.004
92. IRON ORES*R	.035	.021	.006	.008	.000	.000	.012	.006	.008	.000	.010	.010	.065
93. GOLD AND PLATINUM ORES*H	.000	.000	.002	.008	.008	.000	.012	.000	.008	.005	.010	.003	.013
94. CRUDE OIL*R	.002	.002	.000	.001	.002	.008	.003	.004	.004	.002	.009	.005	.001
95. NATURAL GAS*R	.000	.002	.000	.001	.002	.002	.003	.000	.004	.002	.000	.005	.037
96. COAL*R	.000	.000	.000	.000	.000	.002	.000	.000	.000	.000	.002	.001	.000
97. SULPHUR*R	.000	.000	.000	.000	.000	.000	.000	.000	.000	.000	.000	.000	.000
98. ASBESTOS*R	.000	.000	.000	.000	.000	.000	.000	.000	.000	.000	.000	.000	.000
99. SALT AND GYPSUM*R	.000	.005	.001	.000	.000	.002	.001	.000	.000	.000	.002	.000	.002
100. ABRASIVES AND CLAY*R	.001	.001	.000	.000	.000	.001	.001	.001	.000	.000	.001	.000	.002
101. NON-METALLIC MINERALS*R	.000	.000	.000	.000	.000	.000	.000	.000	.001	.000	.001	.001	.001
102. SAND AND GRAVEL*H	.001	.000	.000	.000	.000	.000	.000	.000	.000	.000	.001	.001	.002
103. STONE*R	.001	.000	.000	.000	.000	.002	.000	.002	.000	.000	.000	.001	.000
104. WAGES	.249	.541	.241	.325	.242	.348	.509	.188	.469	.316	.531	.572	.514
105. OTHER VALUE ADDED	.572	.374	.153	.208	.124	.194	.279	.227	.250	.223	.170	.258	.284
106. BALANCE OF TRADE	.000	.000	.000	.000	.000	.000	.000	.000	.000	.000	.000	.000	.000

RESOURCE

	(14)	(15)	(16)	(17)	(18)	(19)	(20)	(21)	(22)	(23)	(24)	(25)	(26)
64. RAW COTTON.NCM	.000	.002	.001	.002	.001	.002	.001	.001	.000	.000	.000	.001	.002
65. RUBBER.NCM	.000	.001	.001	.000	.000	.001	.001	.000	.000	.000	.000	.000	.000
66. CANE SUGAR.NCM	.000	.000	.000	.000	.000	.000	.000	.000	.000	.000	.000	.001	.000
67. COCOA BEANS.NCM	.000	.000	.000	.000	.000	.000	.000	.000	.000	.000	.000	.001	.000
68. GREEN COFFEE.NCM	.000	.000	.000	.001	.001	.001	.000	.001	.000	.000	.000	.001	.000
69. TROPICAL FRUIT.NCM	.000	.000	.000	.000	.000	.000	.000	.000	.000	.000	.000	.000	.000
70. RICE AND HOPS.NCM	.000	.000	.006	.006	.005	.006	.005	.023	.001	.004	.003	.009	.004
71. LIVE ANIMALS.R	.003	.004	.006	.005	.005	.006	.000	.000	.000	.000	.000	.001	.001
72. WHEAT.R	.000	.000	.000	.000	.001	.000	.000	.002	.000	.001	.000	.006	.004
73. OTHER GRAIN.R	.001	.000	.000	.001	.001	.001	.001	.002	.000	.001	.000	.006	.001
74. UNPROCESSED MILK.J	.000	.001	.001	.001	.000	.001	.001	.002	.000	.001	.000	.002	.001
75. EGGS.J	.000	.000	.000	.000	.000	.000	.000	.000	.000	.000	.000	.002	.000
76. HONEY AND BEESWAX.R	.000	.000	.000	.000	.000	.000	.000	.000	.000	.000	.000	.000	.000
77. NUTS, FRUITS, BERRIES.R	.000	.000	.001	.001	.001	.001	.000	.001	.000	.001	.000	.003	.001
78. VEGETABLES.R	.000	.000	.000	.001	.000	.001	.000	.000	.000	.000	.000	.000	.001
79. HAY, GRASS AND NURSERY.R	.000	.000	.000	.000	.000	.000	.001	.000	.000	.000	.000	.000	.000
80. OIL SEEDS AND NUTS.R	.000	.001	.000	.002	.002	.002	.001	.000	.000	.000	.000	.001	.000
81. RAW TOBACCO.R	.000	.000	.000	.000	.000	.000	.000	.000	.000	.000	.000	.000	.000
82. FUR.R	.000	.000	.000	.000	.000	.000	.000	.000	.000	.000	.000	.000	.000
83. WOOL IN THE GREASE.R	.000	.000	.000	.000	.000	.000	.000	.000	.000	.000	.000	.000	.000
84. LOGS AND BOLTS.R	.001	.002	.001	.002	.001	.001	.008	.002	.001	.002	.001	.001	.001
85. POLES AND PIT PROPS.R	.000	.000	.001	.000	.000	.001	.003	.000	.000	.002	.001	.003	.001
86. PULPWOOD.R	.002	.003	.003	.004	.003	.003	.008	.002	.001	.025	.000	.002	.002
87. OTHER CRUDE WOOD.R	.000	.000	.000	.000	.000	.003	.000	.000	.000	.000	.000	.000	.000
88. CUSTOM FORESTRY.J	.000	.000	.000	.000	.000	.000	.000	.000	.000	.000	.000	.000	.000
89. FISH LANDINGS.J	.000	.000	.000	.000	.000	.000	.000	.000	.000	.000	.000	.000	.000
90. METAL ORES.R	.270	.090	.021	.018	.023	.004	.015	.002	.005	.003	.001	.002	.003
91. RADIO-ACTIVE ORES.R	.031	.010	.001	.002	.003	.001	.002	.000	.001	.000	.001	.000	.000
92. IRON ORES.R	.009	.004	.002	.002	.003	.001	.008	.000	.001	.002	.001	.001	.001
93. GOLD AND PLATINUM ORES.R	.005	.000	.017	.015	.043	.012	.016	.016	.004	.037	.004	.006	.009
94. CRUDE OIL.R	.010	.008	.017	.001	.002	.003	.009	.003	.007	.003	.001	.000	.000
95. NATURAL GAS.R	.001	.000	.003	.007	.017	.007	.007	.002	.000	.000	.000	.000	.000
96. COAL.R	.011	.005	.018	.007	.006	.007	.007	.000	.000	.003	.001	.001	.001
97. SULPHUR.R	.000	.000	.000	.004	.004	.004	.000	.000	.000	.000	.000	.000	.000
98. ASBESTOS.R	.000	.000	.000	.000	.001	.001	.000	.000	.000	.000	.000	.000	.000
99. SALT AND GYPSUM.R	.000	.000	.001	.000	.004	.001	.000	.000	.000	.000	.000	.000	.000
100. ABRASIVES AND CLAY.R	.000	.001	.005	.003	.001	.001	.001	.000	.000	.000	.000	.000	.000
101. NON-METALLIC MINERALS.R	.002	.000	.002	.003	.021	.003	.003	.000	.000	.000	.000	.000	.000
102. SAND AND GRAVEL.R	.001	.000	.035	.000	.000	.000	.006	.000	.001	.001	.000	.000	.000
103. STONE.R	.001	.000	.024	.001	.003	.000	.007	.000	.000	.001	.001	.001	.000
104. WAGES	.414	.546	.479	.642	.396	.471	.595	.544	.278	.451	.556	.321	.428
105. OTHER VALUE ADDED	.212	.285	.331	.247	.420	.242	.250	.357	.677	.336	.453	.489	.494
106. BALANCE OF TRADE	.000	.000	.000	.000	.000	.000	.000	.000	.000	.000	.000	.000	.000

TABLE 3.5   RESOURCE REQUIREMENTS PER DOLLAR OF OUTPUT   (CONTINUED)

PRODUCER GROUP*

RESOURCE	(27)	(28)	(29)	(30)	(31)	(32)	(33)	(34)	(35)	(36)	(37)	(38)	(39)
64. RAW COTTON,NCM	.001	.002	.000	.001	.001	.001	.000	.000	.000	.001	.002	.001	.001
65. RUBBER,NCM	.001	.000	.000	.000	.000	.000	.000	.000	.000	.000	.002	.000	.000
66. CANE SUGAR,NCM	.000	.000	.000	.009	.043	.000	.000	.000	.000	.000	.000	.017	.037
67. COCOA BEANS,NCM	.000	.000	.000	.000	.001	.000	.000	.000	.000	.000	.001	.002	.000
68. GREEN COFFEE,NCM	.000	.000	.000	.014	.061	.000	.000	.000	.000	.002	.001	.042	.001
69. TROPICAL FRUIT,NCM	.000	.000	.000	.000	.000	.000	.000	.000	.000	.006	.019	.000	.000
70. RICE AND HOPS,NCM	.008	.000	.012	.001	.006	.003	.000	.000	.000	.006	.001	.000	.004
71. LIVE ANIMALS,NCM	.008	.004	.000	.017	.017	.003	.003	.002	.000	.017	.001	.018	.002
72. WHEAT,R	.001	.000	.000	.274	.012	.000	.000	.000	.000	.034	.001	.016	.011
73. OTHER GRAIN,R	.001	.000	.001	.019	.044	.000	.000	.000	.000	.001	.001	.024	.001
74. UNPROCESSED MILK,P	.003	.001	.001	.006	.004	.001	.001	.000	.000	.001	.004	.009	.001
75. EGGS,P	.001	.000	.000	.002	.002	.000	.000	.000	.000	.000	.001	.002	.000
76. HONEY AND BEESWAX,P	.000	.000	.003	.000	.003	.145	.000	.000	.000	.000	.000	.000	.130
77. NUTS, FRUITS, BERRIES,P	.001	.000	.000	.003	.003	.000	.000	.000	.000	.000	.001	.000	.000
78. VEGETABLES,R	.001	.001	.000	.000	.018	.140	.000	.000	.000	.000	.002	.048	.048
79. HAY, GRASS AND NURSERY,R	.000	.000	.003	.006	.002	.000	.000	.000	.001	.001	.001	.057	.057
80. OIL SEEDS AND NUTS,R	.001	.001	.000	.000	.008	.001	.000	.000	.000	.000	.001	.000	.001
81. RAW TOBACCO,P	.000	.000	.000	.005	.000	.000	.000	.000	.000	.000	.000	.000	.000
82. FUR,P	.000	.000	.000	.000	.000	.000	.000	.000	.000	.000	.000	.000	.000
83. WOOL IN THE GREASE,R	.007	.000	.000	.000	.001	.000	.000	.000	.000	.002	.000	.000	.002
84. LOGS AND BOLTS,R	.007	.010	.001	.002	.001	.000	.001	.000	.001	.000	.003	.002	.002
85. POLES AND PIT PROPS,P	.000	.000	.000	.001	.000	.000	.000	.000	.000	.002	.000	.000	.000
86. PULPWOOD,R	.010	.000	.003	.000	.006	.000	.001	.001	.005	.008	.006	.000	.006
87. OTHER CRUDE WOOD,P	.000	.117	.000	.008	.001	.000	.000	.000	.000	.000	.000	.000	.000
88. CUSTOM FORESTRY,P	.000	.000	.000	.000	.001	.000	.000	.000	.000	.000	.000	.000	.000
89. FISH LANDINGS,P	.003	.000	.509	.000	.001	.000	.000	.000	.000	.004	.001	.001	.000
90. METAL ORES,R	.003	.005	.004	.002	.003	.003	.048	.492	.019	.001	.009	.007	.002
91. RADIO-ACTIVE ORES,R	.001	.001	.001	.001	.001	.001	.007	.056	.002	.001	.001	.001	.001
92. IRON ORES,R	.000	.001	.001	.000	.001	.000	.110	.003	.001	.001	.003	.000	.007
93. GOLD AND PLATINUM ORES,R	.000	.000	.007	.000	.000	.000	.000	.011	.041	.009	.014	.009	.007
94. CRUDE OIL,R	.018	.013	.000	.010	.020	.009	.015	.011	.002	.000	.000	.001	.004
95. NATURAL GAS,R	.001	.001	.000	.001	.001	.001	.021	.011	.016	.000	.004	.004	.004
96. COAL,P	.002	.009	.002	.002	.003	.009	.060	.001	.006	.004	.004	.000	.000
97. SULPHUR,R	.000	.003	.000	.000	.000	.003	.000	.001	.000	.000	.000	.000	.000
98. ASBESTOS,P	.000	.001	.000	.000	.000	.000	.000	.001	.004	.001	.000	.000	.002
99. SALT AND GYPSUM,P	.000	.001	.002	.001	.001	.000	.000	.001	.000	.001	.000	.001	.001
100. ABRASIVES AND CLAY,R	.000	.002	.000	.000	.001	.001	.002	.002	.001	.001	.000	.001	.001
101. NON-METALLIC MINERALS,R	.000	.000	.000	.000	.001	.002	.001	.002	.036	.001	.001	.000	.001
102. SAND AND GRAVEL,R	.000	.002	.000	.000	.001	.001	.001	.001	.001	.001	.001	.001	.001
103. STONE,R	.000	.002	.000	.000	.001	.001	.003	.003	.003	.001	.001	.001	.001
104. WAGES	.453	.473	.324	.390	.296	.375	.413	.252	.407	.410	.533	.398	.357
105. OTHER VALUE ADDED	.371	.314	.105	.192	.400	.276	.244	.146	.400	.431	.331	.267	.389
106. BALANCE OF TRADE	.000	.000	.000	.000	.000	.000	.000	.000	.000	.000	.000	.000	.000

TABLE 3.5   RESOURCE REQUIREMENTS PER DOLLAR OF OUTPUT   (CONTINUED)

PRODUCER GROUP*

RESOURCE	(40)	(41)	(42)	(43)	(44)	(45)	(46)	(47)	(48)	(49)	(50)	(51)	(52)
64. RAW COTTON,NCM	.021	.008	.221	.041	.039	.001	.000	.001	.000	.001	.001	.003	.002
65. RUBBER,NCM	.057	.004	.001	.000	.001	.000	.001	.000	.000	.001	.001	.003	.002
66. CANE SUGAR,NCM	.000	.000	.000	.000	.000	.000	.000	.000	.000	.000	.000	.000	.000
67. COCOA BEANS,NCM	.000	.001	.000	.000	.000	.000	.000	.000	.000	.000	.000	.000	.000
68. GREEN COFFEE,NCM	.001	.001	.000	.000	.000	.000	.000	.000	.000	.000	.001	.000	.000
69. TROPICAL FRUIT,NCM	.000	.000	.000	.000	.000	.000	.000	.000	.000	.000	.000	.000	.000
70. RICE AND HOPS,NCM	.000	.000	.004	.005	.006	.003	.004	.004	.004	.004	.003	.005	.004
71. LIVE ANIMALS,R	.005	.050	.000	.000	.000	.000	.000	.000	.000	.000	.000	.000	.000
72. WHEAT,R	.000	.001	.000	.001	.000	.000	.000	.000	.000	.000	.000	.000	.000
73. OTHER GRAIN,R	.000	.001	.001	.001	.001	.001	.001	.001	.001	.001	.001	.001	.001
74. UNPROCESSED MILK,R	.000	.000	.000	.000	.000	.000	.000	.000	.000	.000	.000	.000	.000
75. EGGS,P	.000	.000	.000	.000	.000	.000	.000	.000	.000	.000	.000	.000	.000
76. HONEY AND BEESWAX,R	.000	.000	.000	.000	.000	.000	.000	.000	.000	.000	.000	.000	.000
77. NUTS, FRUITS, BERRIES,R	.000	.000	.001	.000	.001	.001	.001	.000	.000	.000	.000	.000	.000
78. VEGETABLES,R	.001	.001	.001	.000	.001	.000	.001	.000	.000	.000	.000	.000	.000
79. HAY, GRASS AND NURSERY,R	.001	.001	.001	.001	.001	.001	.001	.000	.000	.000	.000	.001	.000
80. OIL SEEDS AND NUTS,R	.001	.001	.000	.000	.000	.000	.001	.000	.000	.000	.000	.000	.000
81. RAW TOBACCO,R	.001	.001	.000	.001	.001	.000	.001	.000	.000	.000	.000	.000	.000
82. FIBRE,U	.001	.001	.003	.002	.019	.000	.000	.000	.000	.000	.000	.001	.000
83. WOOL IN THE GREASE,R	.001	.001	.011	.060	.004	.000	.000	.000	.000	.000	.001	.001	.000
84. LOGS AND BOLTS,R	.001	.002	.001	.001	.002	.019	.001	.001	.001	.002	.000	.001	.003
85. POLES AND PIT PROPS,R	.004	.005	.003	.003	.004	.027	.002	.003	.002	.004	.002	.003	.004
86. PULPWOOD,R	.004	.000	.003	.003	.000	.000	.000	.000	.000	.000	.000	.000	.000
87. OTHER CRUDE WOOD,R	.000	.000	.000	.000	.000	.000	.000	.000	.000	.000	.000	.000	.000
88. CUSTOM FORESTRY,P	.000	.001	.000	.000	.000	.000	.001	.000	.000	.000	.000	.000	.000
89. FISH LANDINGS,R	.007	.003	.002	.003	.003	.004	.142	.071	.032	.023	.016	.016	.020
90. METAL ORES,P	.001	.003	.000	.003	.003	.000	.016	.008	.003	.002	.002	.002	.002
91. RADIO-ACTIVE ORES,R	.001	.001	.002	.001	.001	.004	.070	.016	.003	.013	.006	.007	.002
92. IRON ORES,R	.000	.001	.000	.001	.001	.000	.017	.009	.000	.009	.010	.008	.012
93. GOLD AND PLATINUM ORES,R	.000	.008	.000	.007	.008	.007	.041	.000	.000	.009	.010	.008	.009
94. CRUDE OIL,R	.011	.008	.006	.007	.008	.000	.001	.000	.012	.010	.005	.008	.001
95. NATURAL GAS,R	.000	.000	.000	.000	.000	.000	.001	.001	.001	.000	.000	.000	.010
96. COAL,P	.007	.004	.007	.008	.004	.003	.001	.012	.028	.010	.000	.001	.000
97. SULPHUR,R	.002	.000	.000	.000	.000	.001	.002	.000	.000	.000	.001	.000	.001
98. ASBESTOS,R	.001	.000	.000	.000	.000	.000	.002	.000	.000	.000	.000	.000	.010
99. SALT AND GYPSUM,R	.000	.001	.000	.000	.000	.000	.001	.001	.001	.003	.001	.001	.000
100. ABRASIVES AND CLAY,R	.001	.000	.000	.000	.000	.000	.001	.001	.001	.001	.000	.000	.000
101. NON-METALLIC MINERALS,P	.003	.001	.001	.001	.001	.000	.002	.001	.001	.001	.001	.001	.001
102. SAND AND GRAVEL,P	.000	.001	.001	.000	.001	.001	.002	.001	.001	.001	.001	.001	.001
103. STONE,P	.001	.001	.000	.000	.000	.000	.002	.001	.001	.000	.001	.001	.001
104. WAGES	.523	.478	.500	.594	.629	.422	.391	.561	.554	.606	.718	.572	.527
105. OTHER VALUE ADDED	.712	.189	.219	.238	.241	.274	.276	.273	.274	.279	.191	.321	.257
106. BALANCE OF TRADE	.000	.000	.000	.000	.000	.000	.000	.000	.000	.000	.000	.000	.000

TABLE 3.5 RESOURCE REQUIREMENTS PER DOLLAR OF OUTPUT (CONTINUED)

RESOURCE

PRODUCER GROUPS*

		(53)	(54)	(55)	(56)	(57)	(58)	(59)	(60)	(61)	(62)	(63)
64.	RAW COTTON.NCM	.001	.001	.003	.000	.002	.001	.001	.001	.001	.004	.004
65.	RUBBER.NCM	.001	.001	.001	.000	.001	.001	.001	.001	.000	.003	.004
66.	CANE SUGAR.NCM	.000	.000	.000	.000	.002	.001	.001	.000	.000	.000	.000
67.	COCOA BEANS.NCM	.000	.000	.000	.000	.003	.001	.002	.000	.000	.001	.000
68.	GREEN COFFEE.NCM	.000	.000	.000	.000	.000	.000	.000	.000	.000	.000	.000
69.	TROPICAL FRUIT.NCM	.000	.000	.000	.000	.015	.000	.002	.000	.000	.000	.000
70.	RICE AND HOPS.NCM	.003	.004	.005	.003	.015	.015	.006	.004	.004	.021	.008
71.	LIVE ANIMALS.R	.000	.000	.000	.000	.002	.001	.001	.001	.000	.001	.000
72.	WHEAT.R	.000	.000	.000	.000	.003	.001	.001	.000	.000	.001	.001
73.	OTHER GRAIN.R	.000	.001	.000	.000	.002	.000	.000	.000	.000	.000	.001
74.	UNPROCESSED MILK.R	.000	.000	.000	.000	.000	.000	.000	.000	.000	.000	.000
75.	EGGS.R	.000	.000	.000	.000	.000	.000	.000	.000	.000	.000	.000
76.	HONEY AND BEESWAX.R	.000	.000	.000	.000	.000	.000	.000	.000	.000	.000	.000
77.	NUTS, FRUITS, BERRIES.R	.000	.000	.000	.000	.002	.001	.001	.000	.000	.000	.001
78.	VEGETABLES.R	.000	.000	.000	.000	.003	.000	.001	.002	.000	.001	.000
79.	HAY, GRASS AND NURSERY.R	.001	.001	.001	.000	.000	.002	.001	.000	.001	.001	.001
80.	OIL SEEDS AND NUTS.R	.000	.000	.000	.000	.004	.016	.003	.001	.000	.000	.000
81.	RAW TOBACCO.R	.000	.001	.001	.000	.000	.000	.003	.000	.000	.005	.001
82.	FUR.R	.000	.000	.000	.000	.000	.000	.000	.000	.000	.000	.000
83.	WOOL IN THE GREASE.R	.000	.000	.000	.000	.000	.000	.000	.000	.000	.000	.001
84.	LOGS AND BOLTS.R	.002	.002	.002	.001	.002	.003	.002	.002	.001	.003	.006
85.	POLES AND PIT PROPS.R	.002	.000	.000	.000	.000	.000	.001	.000	.003	.000	.001
86.	PULPWOOD.R	.003	.003	.004	.001	.009	.007	.005	.004	.003	.011	.009
87.	OTHER CRUDE WOOD.R	.000	.000	.000	.000	.000	.000	.000	.000	.000	.000	.000
88.	CUSTOM FORESTRY.J	.000	.000	.000	.000	.003	.000	.000	.000	.000	.000	.000
89.	FISH LANDINGS.R	.000	.000	.000	.006	.005	.001	.012	.000	.000	.008	.000
90.	METAL ORES.R	.012	.024	.012	.003	.015	.015	.012	.023	.039	.001	.010
91.	RADIO-ACTIVE ORES.R	.001	.003	.001	.001	.001	.002	.002	.003	.004	.001	.004
92.	IRON ORES.R	.010	.010	.002	.000	.001	.002	.002	.005	.004	.001	.003
93.	GOLD AND PLATINUM ORES.R	.007	.001	.017	.575	.013	.030	.034	.007	.070	.017	.011
94.	CRUDE OIL.R	.000	.000	.002	.000	.001	.001	.002	.000	.006	.000	.000
95.	NATURAL GAS.R	.008	.007	.009	.002	.005	.004	.012	.005	.005	.006	.005
96.	COAL.R	.000	.000	.001	.000	.001	.002	.004	.000	.000	.001	.000
97.	SULPHUR.R	.000	.000	.019	.000	.001	.000	.003	.001	.000	.000	.000
98.	ASBESTOS.R	.001	.001	.005	.001	.003	.004	.013	.001	.001	.004	.001
99.	SALT AND GYPSUM.R	.000	.001	.011	.001	.001	.001	.001	.001	.001	.001	.000
100.	ABRASIVES AND CLAY.R	.001	.001	.005	.001	.003	.002	.013	.001	.001	.004	.001
101.	NON-METALLIC MINERALS.R	.000	.001	.004	.001	.001	.001	.002	.001	.001	.001	.001
102.	SAND AND GRAVEL.R	.001	.001	.012	.001	.001	.001	.002	.001	.001	.001	.001
103.	STONE.R	.012	.011	.550	.174	.512	.468	.425	.585	.547	.548	.583
104.	WAGES	.699	.646	.550	.174	.512	.468	.425	.585	.547	.548	.583
105.	OTHER VALUE ADDED	.217	.250	.223	.217	.350	.361	.417	.313	.240	.315	.296
106.	BALANCE OF TRADE	.000	.000	.000	.000	.000	.000	.000	.000	.000	.000	.000

constrained to be imported or domestic and commodities that are domestic in 1961 are constrained to remain domestic or to be imported. These assumptions are incorporated in the problem format by simply omitting certain import and export vectors.

In the empirical version of the model, units of quantity and units of foreign exchange have been defined such that all prices and the exchange rate in the initial situation are equal to one. This is particularly convenient because, under these circumstances, the *ad valorem* US tariff is equivalent to the specific tariff required by the model. Recall from equation (2.1) of chapter two that the equilibrium condition with regard to exports is

$$p_{1j} + rs_{2j} \geqslant rp_{2j}.$$

If $s_{2j}{}^*$ is the *ad valorem* tariff this same condition would be written

$$p_{1j} + rp_{1j}s_{2j}{}^* \geqslant rp_{2j},$$

which is the same as the preceding expression if the exchange rate, r, and all p_{1j} are equal to unity. The relationship between the Canadian specific and *ad valorem* tariff is somewhat more complicated.

If $s_{ij}{}^*$ is the *ad valorem* tariff, the specific tariff can be computed from the formula

$$s_{1j} = s_{1j}{}^* / (1 + s_{1j}{}^*). \tag{3.1}$$

This is justified as follows. The equilibrium condition with regard to imports was given by expression (2.2) in chapter two as

$$rp_{2j} \geqslant p_{1j} - s_{1j}. \tag{3.2}$$

In *ad valorem* terms this expression will be written

$$rp_{2j} \geqslant p_{1j} - rs_{1j}{}^*p_{2j}. \tag{3.3}$$

If $p_{1j} = 1$ for all j, it is clear that expressions (3.2) and (3.3) are equivalent when s_{1j} is computed as indicated in expression (3.1). Rearrange expression (3.1) to read $s_{1j}{}^* = s_{1j}/(1 - s_{1j})$, and substitute into (3.3). Assuming $(1 - s_{1j}) \geqslant 0$, we obtain

$$rp_{2j} \geqslant p_{1j} - p_{1j}s_{1j}.$$

This is the same expression (3.2), provided all $p_{1j} = 1$. Canadian specific tariffs are computed using (3.1).

THE COST OF THE TARIFF

In estimating the cost of the tariff the ten per cent restrictions on output variation are removed and the increased amount of the composite commodity made available is determined. The cost of the tariff is equal to the difference between the value of the composite commodity in free trade and the value of the composite commodity under restricted trade. In measuring the cost of the tariff we are no longer concerned with determining what *will happen* in free trade. The objective is to find the best technically possible alternative to re-stricted trade. This is done by setting all tariffs and taxes in the linear programming format at zero. The interpretation of the outcome has already been discussed in chapter one.

There are no conclusions to this chapter. The most general conclusions have already been given in chapter one and the particular applications to the various sectors of the Canadian economy are the subject matter of part two.

PART TWO

In the remaining chapters of this book the quantitative results of part one are used to analyse the effects of the Canadian-US tariff in various industrial sectors. The data for each sector are organized into three summary tables.

The first summary table of each chapter is concerned with the relationship of each producer classification to the main divisions of the economy. The percentage of output shipped as intermediate goods to other producers is shown in column 3 of this table. Column 4 gives the ratio of value added to total output. The ratio of net trade to output is displayed in column 5. From columns 6, 7, and 8 the reader can determine the percentage of cost spent respectively in the domestic, export, and import competing sectors of the economy. In column 9 the percentage of cost spent for resource commodities is given. In order to give some indication of the size of each producer classification, we show total value added and total output in columns one and two of the first summary table.

In the second table of each chapter data on tariffs, taxes, and transport costs are found. Column 1 shows taxes per dollar of output and column 2 indicates transport costs per dollar of output. The US tariff as of 1961 is given in column 3 and the Canadian tariff as of 1961 is displayed in column 4. The level of the Canadian tariff after the Kennedy Round is shown in column 5.

The effect of the Canadian and US tariff on the cost of intermediate goods purchased by each producer classification can be determined from columns 6 and 7 of the second table of each chapter. We refer to the values shown in columns 6 and 7 of this table as the cost per dollar of output because they indicate the amount that the costs of a producer have been increased due to the Canadian and US tariff schedules. The last column of the second table in each chapter shows the percentage change necessary for each producer group to reach the optimal level indicated by the linear programming algorithm. The algebraic sign in the column is more significant than the indicated magnitude. If the sign is positive, it means that the net effect of the tariff was to reduce the relative size of that producer classification compared to the size it would reach in free trade. Under free trade relative prices the group would expand. If the sign is negative, it indicates that, at free trade relative prices, the producer group would decline.

The third and last table of each chapter shows the percentage of cost in each producer classification which is used to purchase intermediate goods from every other producer classification in the same sector.

4

The iron and steel sector

The Canadian tariff schedule is intended to favour manufacturing of products which are at a finished or nearly finished stage of processing relative to production of goods at earlier stages. If the tariff rates which apply to commodities are appropriately adjusted, it should be possible for the government to achieve this objective by raising the prices of end products relative to the prices of intermediate goods. In the iron and steel sector this strategy has not been successful. In many cases the tariff seems to have had exactly the opposite effect. It is therefore possible to make marginal adjustments in the tariff which will simultaneously move Canada more in the direction of greater processing and more toward an allocation of production which is in line with Canada's comparative advantage.

PRODUCERS OF IRON AND STEEL INTERMEDIATE PRODUCTS

The classification system employed in this chapter as elsewhere is a consequence of the aggregation procedures discussed in chapter one. In the iron and steel sector it is necessary to define classifications for intermediate products in each of the major sectors of the economy. Domestic producers are aggregated in group 13 where, as a consequence, the ratio of net trade to production is less than one per cent. This should be compared to the ratio of net trade to output which holds in the case of group 33. By aggregating the producers with exportable output in group 33, it was possible to form a classification where the ratio of net exports to output was 0.496. Import competing producers of iron and steel intermediate products are aggregated in group 48 where the ratio of net imports to production is −0.235. The producers in each of the iron and steel intermediate products groups purchases iron ore (92) which is processed at one stage or another for shipment to producers within the iron and steel sector and

TABLE 4.1

Summary of data relating to value added trade and shipments of output from certain sectors to producers in the iron and steel sector

Name of producer group	Value added (1)	Total output (2)	Percentage intermediate shipments (3)	Ratio VA/TO (4)	Ratio Trade/TO (5)	Proportion of costs used to purchase[1] D (6)	E (7)	M (8)	R (9)
13 Iron and steel intermediates, D	330,754	762,478	98.0	0.424	−0.009	0.188	0.147	0.143	0.087
33 Iron and steel intermediates, E	42,850	98,160	98.6	0.427	0.496	0.100	0.185	0.080	0.198
48 Iron and steel intermediates, M	434,702	1,032,196	96.4	0.410	−0.235	0.200	0.117	0.207	0.055
49 Machinery and equipment, M	406,798	879,389	39.4	0.450	−0.874	0.215	0.064	0.248	0.011
50 Aircraft, including parts, M	165,550	347,544	20.5	0.462	−0.230	0.139	0.063	0.321	0.001
51 Autos, trucks, and parts, M	377,689	1,207,123	34.0	0.302	−0.447	0.136	0.053	0.496	0.002
52 Buses and locomotives, M	15,615	43,651	25.0	0.346	−0.239	0.192	0.075	0.374	0.002
53 Transportation equipment, M	76,656	141,027	6.2	0.533	−0.121	0.138	0.042	0.275	0.001

1 D refers to the domestic sector, E refers to the export sector, M refers to the import competing sector, and R refers to resource purchases.

TABLE 4.2

Summary of tariffs and other data for the iron and steel sector[1]

Name of producer group	Taxes and government subsidies (1)	Transportation costs (2)	US tariff before Kennedy Round (3)	Canadian tariff		Cost Effect Per Dollar of TO		Percentage change in output required to reach optimal level of production (8)
				Before Kennedy Round (4)	After Kennedy Round (5)	Before Kennedy Round (6)	After Kennedy Round (7)	
13 Iron and steel intermediates, D	0.010	0.028	0.055	0.094	0.084	−0.014	−0.013	+1.16
33 Iron and steel intermediates, E	0.010	0.027	0.031	0.026	0.026	−0.006	−0.006	+10.0
48 Iron and steel intermediates, M	0.011	0.028	0.043	0.143	0.124	−0.022	−0.021	−3.76
49 Machinery and equipment, M	0.013	0.028	0.064	0.110	0.101	−0.024	−0.025	−10.0
50 Aircraft Including parts, M	0.015	0.019	0.104	0.051	0.078	−0.035	−0.031	10.0
51 Autos, trucks, and parts, M	0.011	0.032	0.052	0.098	0.081	−0.066	−0.051	10.0
52 Buses and locomotives, M	0.012	0.039	0.124	0.128	0.091	−0.048	−0.040	10.0
53 Transportation equipment, M	0.011	0.028	0.039	0.147	0.120	−0.029	−0.028	10.0

1 See note to Table 4.1.

TABLE 4.3

Shipments among industries in the iron and steel sector[1]

Industry originating shipments	Industry receiving shipments							
	(13)	(33)	(48)	(49)	(50)	(51)	(52)	(53)
13 Iron and steel intermediates, D	0.096	0.020	0.101	0.097	0.039	0.037	0.077	0.046
33 Iron and steel intermediates, E	0.022	0.017	0.015	0.002	0.001	0.001	0.002	0.000
48 Iron and steel intermediates, M	0.064	0.026	0.125	0.074	0.021	0.020	0.072	0.107
49 Machinery and equipment, M	0.012	0.008	0.011	0.088	0.013	0.005	0.021	0.079
50 Aircraft including parts, M	0.001	0.000	0.001	0.000	0.187	0.000	0.000	0.000
51 Autos, trucks, and parts, M	0.004	0.000	0.001	0.007	0.005	0.345	0.134	0.004
52 Buses and locomotives, M	0.000	0.000	0.000	0.000	0.000	0.006	0.005	0.000
53 Transportation equipment, M	0.000	0.000	0.000	0.000	0.000	0.000	0.000	0.008
92 Iron ore, R	0.052	0.105	0.033	0.001	0.000	0.000	0.000	0.000

1 See note to Table 4.1.

to many producers outside this sector. Of the latter, producers of non-ferrous metal products are most notable.

The exportable iron and steel products of group 33 have passed through only the first stages of iron and steel intermediate processing. Output consists of basic products such as pig iron, iron and steel ingots, blooms, billets, and slabs. This is also the group which uses the largest percentage of its costs to purchase resource commodities. About one-half of this or ten per cent of costs is used to purchase iron ore (92). The remainder is used mostly to purchase coal (96) or metal ores (90). Iron and steel intermediate (13) products produced for the domestic market are next highest in the order of processing. Only nine per cent of the costs of these producers is used to purchase resources. Output consists of such items as steel bars, rods, railway tracks, pipes, tanks, and boilers. Such commodities represent a level of processing that is higher than in the classification producing exportable commodities but not as near end product production as are the products of the iron and steel intermediate group (48) which is the import competing class. Here the percentage of cost used to purchase resources is only 5.5 and the type of product manufactured is more sophisticated. The output of the import competing producers will have been punched, drilled, or otherwise fabricated. It will include scaffolding equipment, prefabricated metal buildings, fabricated or coated steel strips, heating equipment, plumbing equipment, safes and vaults. This represents a typical Canadian pattern. The export sector, group 33, is engaged at the initial stage of processing while the import competing sector, group 48, is engaged at the latest stages of processing, with the domestic sector, group 13, falling in between these extremes.

In a simulation in which the Canadian tariff and taxes were set at zero, it was found that producers in the domestic and import competing groups would expand relative to producers in the export group and, hence, that later stage processing would expand relative to the earlier stages. This may be explained, in part, by referring to Table 4.1. Producers of exportable iron and steel intermediate (33) products use only eight per cent of their costs to purchase intermediate goods from the import competing sector of the economy. With the Canadian tariff eliminated the price of many types of intermediate goods in this class will decline by the amount of the Canadian tariff but the reductions will apply to only a small portion of the total costs of the export industries (33). In the domestic group (13) and the import competing group (48) the percentage of cost used to purchase goods from the domestic and import competing sector of the economy are larger than in the export group (33). With the Canadian tariff eliminated, the level of antiprotection is significantly reduced and relative prices in the domestic sector may also decline. This change improves the competitive position of the domestic and import competing groups relative to producers in group 33 who have exportable output.

In the simulation in which *both* the Canadian and the American tariff were eliminated we find that the export classification 33 has expanded while the import cometing group 48 has contracted. This would represent a shift toward earlier stages of processing compensated, however, by expansion in the domestic classification 13. The higher prices obtainable under free trade for Canadian exports shipped to the United States leads to expansion at the earlier stage of processing, costs rise at the later stage represented by the import competing classification 48.

The direct protection of the Canadian tariff is highest where it is most needed and rises with the degree of processing. In the import competing group (48) the pre-Kennedy average Canadian tariff was 14.3 per cent, in the domestic sector the pre-Kennedy tariff was 9.4 per cent and in the export sector only 2.6 per cent. The US tariff is lowest for Canadian exportable iron and steel products and highest on goods produced by the domestic group (13) of the iron and steel intermediate sector.

A certain portion of the iron and steel sector has been studied in more detail by Eastman and Stykolt (1967, 337-63). These authors were particularly concerned with the question of economies of scale in iron and steel production. They found (page 353) that steel smelting was generally of efficient size in Canada but that blast furnace and rolling mill operations were at too small a scale to be efficient. The simulation indicates that Canadian output would expand relatively at the pig iron and steel smelting stage accompanied by expansion of products from the finishing mills. The result is derived under the assumption that there are constant returns to scale and no attempt was made to take account of technological relationships which can exist between smelting and mill production. With free trade and the possibility of exploiting the US market, economies of scale would come into operation and output at the rolling and finishing level would be more encouraged than indicated by the simulation.

The costs of one of the producers in the domestic group (13) of the iron and steel intermediate products group has been studied in detail by Wonnacott and Wonnacott (1967, 261). The authors conclude on the basis of observed prices that the output of steel pipes and tubes could not become an exportable product under free trade but that the present levels of production in the Canadian domestic market could be maintained if these producers could reach the US level of efficiency. The authors express some doubt, however, that this would be possible in the Canadian context and hence are somewhat more pessimistic than is warranted on the basis of the simulation results. In the simulation relative prices in Canada are allowed to vary and the simulation indicates that this change would favour the producers in the domestic group (13).

The groups producing iron and steel intermediate products are important suppliers to each other and to producer groups inside and outside the iron and steel sector. Many of the firms which purchase iron and steel intermediate products are themselves producers of iron and steel intermediate products and, due to the higher costs in Canada of intermediate products, must be protected to compensate for the antiprotection passed on from the lower stages of processing. The antiprotection generated at the earlier stages escalates to later stages. The simulation indicates that all of the end product producers in the iron and steel sector would expand under free trade pricing. It is of great importance, therefore, that the general level of antiprotection should be reduced. Ironically, the iron and steel producers are themselves victims of the antiprotection they generate and of the antiprotection generated in the non-ferrous metals group. If the Canadian tariff protection were removed without reducing the level of antiprotection it would cause distress in some lines of production which would or could be competitive under free trade pricing.

The domestic producers of group 13 in the period prior to the Kennedy Round faced the highest US tariff. Reductions in the US tariff might bring about adjustment in the direction of comparative advantage. The US tariff is of lesser importance as far as the import competing producers of group 48 are concerned because there is little export potential with or without the tariff. In the chapters that follow it will become more apparent that classification 48 is a significant source of antiprotection in other producer groups.

MACHINERY AND EQUIPMENT

The ratio of imports to production in the machinery and equipment (49) producer group is −0.874. Despite this large flow of imports, Canadian production is not small. The value of output in 1961 was greater than the value of output in the autos, trucks, and parts (51) producer group. Machinery and equipment (49) producers are very important as suppliers[1] to other producers and, because of the large flow of imports, we may assume that the Canadian cost of production is higher in the US and that, therefore, the price exceeds the US price by an amount equal to the Canadian tariff in many product lines.

Machinery and equipment (49) is a very heterogeneous classification. Imports are protected by a number of tariff items. In the pre-Kennedy period the applicable tariff depended in many cases on the productive use to be made of the imported machine or piece of equipment. Certain producers were allowed to import machines of a particular type 'for use in their own factories' at a rate of duty lower than would be charged to other producers. Some tariff items restricted this privilege to machines 'not of a class or kind made in Canada.' In certain cases a machine could be imported duty free if it met either or both of these qualifications but more typically a most favoured nation rate of 22.5 per cent applied if the import did not qualify, and a most favoured nation rate of

7.5 applied if the import did qualify. It was an administrative rule of thumb that, in order for a commodity to qualify as of a class and kind not made in Canada, Canadian production had to be less than ten per cent of Canadian sales.

Masson and English (1963, 20) comment that the 'made in Canada' condition is a perverse type of protection. It gives no protection to a developing line of production unless it should reach a size large enough to establish its market position and perhaps realize economies of scale. At this point it is awarded tariff protection which it thereafter can use as a shield for its own inefficiency or for monopolistic pricing. From the point of view of firms buying machines, nothing could be worse. The cost of machines previously imported may suddenly cost one-fifth more if they are found to be of a class and kind made in Canada. The Canadian variety of the machine, although of the same class and kind, might not be suitable for a particular use and, in any case, producers who switch over to the Canadian variety of the machine will have the additional cost of retraining personnel to maintain and use the equipment.

During the Kennedy Round the Canadian government pledged itself to replace tariff items in the machinery and equipment class with a single tariff item which would apply to most imports. After the Kennedy Round a most favoured nation rate of fifteen per cent was to apply on all such machines but a full rebate could be obtained if an import qualified as not made in Canada. A board was to be established which would recommend full remission of duty to qualified imports on a case by case basis (Department of Trade and Commerce, 1967, 41). Canada pledged that the number of remissions would be sufficient to keep the average duty on machines below nine per cent, however. To the extent that it fails to take account of this more liberal rebate policy, the rather small calculated reduction in the average rate of duty on machines and equipment shown in column 5 of Table 6.2 slightly underestimates the actual size of the Kennedy Round reduction. Also, the new system will rely on administrative judgment rather than on a legal interpretation of prescribed rules and this is expected to reduce the amount of litigation and to speed up the time needed to obtain rulings. The new administrative machinery will do very little to alter the perverse nature of the 'made in Canada' clause, however. Any firms which can qualify under the new administrative rules will be entitled to protection but the level of protection will be reduced to fifteen per cent.

Producers of machinery and equipment (49) are at a stage of processing between producers of iron and steel intermediate products and producers of end products. Very little is spent on resource purchases, but a large percentage of costs are used to purchase the output of intermediate iron and steel producers. Machinery and equipment (49) producers are important suppliers to many end product producers and therefore become a channel through which costs become escalated at the end product stage. Twenty-five per cent of costs are used to purchase goods from the import competing sector but only six per cent of costs are used to purchase goods from the export sector. The level of antiprotection is equal to -2.5 per cent of cost. Free trade pricing would eliminate this antiprotection, but, according to the simulation, this would not be sufficient to overcome the loss of direct protection. The machinery and equipment (49) producer groups would be expected to decline relative to other groups in the iron and steel sector.

It is clear from the simulation and from the large volume of imports that Canadian production of machinery and equipment was at too high a level relative to output in other industries in 1961. The tariff protection which encouraged this outcome is a cause of antiprotection in many other producer groups. The tariff raises the costs of machines in Canada and the Canadian producer is thereby forced to raise prices or to depreciate his equipment over a longer period than his foreign rivals. Since new machines embody the latest technological advances, the Canadian rate of technological growth is itself inhibited. In order to minimize cost, Canadian producers need to have machines of precisely the right variety. If a machine is declared to be 'of a class and kind made in Canada' the producer must either choose a Canadian machine which is not suitable for the task or pay the higher cost of importing the foreign product. The tariff schedule itself is evidence that the matter is a serious concern to producers[2] who purchase imported machines.

END PRODUCTS OF IRON AND STEEL

The four end product producers in the iron and steel sector are aircraft including parts (50), autos, trucks, and parts (51), buses and locomotives (52), and transportation equipment (53). End product producers use from six to fifteen per cent of costs to purchase the output of the iron and steel intermediate sector and additional percentages are used to purchase machinery and equipment. Insofar as these are more costly in Canada, the end product producers are at a disadvantage in competition with imports and in 1961 each of these producers faced considerable import competition. The ratio of net imports to output varied from twelve to forty-five per cent. Because of the large volume of imports, it may be assumed that costs are generally higher in Canada than in the United States and it will be frequently necessary for Canadian firms to set their price above the US price by the amount of the Canadian tariff. We learn from the simulation that, although the full amount of tariff protection was needed in 1961, no protection would have been required under free trade pricing. In the simulation each producer class expands by the maximum amount permitted by the algorithm.

Purchases of the end product producers are concentrated on the import competing sector of the economy where twenty-eight to fifty percent of costs are used. Purchases from the export sector never rise above eight per cent. Consequently, the computed amount of antiprotection is very high. Under free trade pricing this antiprotection would disappear. In addition, there might be a reduction in the relative prices of goods purchased from the domestic sector which also accounts for a substantial portion of the costs of end product producers. Although the simulation implies that these end product producers can be strong competitors under free trade pricing, the existing tariffs which apply in the end product classification cannot be reduced unless the present levels of antiprotection are also reduced simultaneously. None of the end product producers is itself a cause of antiprotection and, therefore, the Canadian tariff protection is of less concern because it causes little cost distortion in the rest of the economy.

The reader may have observed that the Canadian tariff applicable to the aircraft including parts (50) producer group is higher after the Kennedy Round than before. This is not due to tariff increases after the Kennedy Round; it is due to a tariff increase on 1 July 1967. Tariff items 44043-1 and 44047-1 were increased in 1967 and then reduced from this higher rate during the Kennedy Round. The Kennedy Round reduction was not large enough to bring the rate back to the level prior to 1967.

There are certain special features of the autos, trucks, and parts (51) producer group that also require some attention. Nearly thirty-five per cent of the purchases of these producers are made from other producers in the same group. As in the case of the paper products (28) producers discussed in a later chapter, the autos, trucks, and parts (51) classification aggregates together producer groups at several stages of processing. The extent of this is not exceeded in any other classification. The ratio of net imports to production of autos, trucks, and parts (51) in 1961 was -0.447. The 1964 trade data show that Canada was a net importer in every single classification at the level of the import commodity code. This is an obvious case where a preference for producers at one stage of processing would necessarily conflict with the interest of producers at other stages. Under such conditions a difficult political decision is involved and the government found a political solution. A 'class and kind' clause gave protection to existing producers whether or not they produced efficiently and duty remission on intermediate goods not produced in Canada was offered as a means of promoting Canada as a location for certain end product production (Beigie, 1970, chap. 1) which would otherwise be located in the US. Producers who were thus attracted to Canada could continue to compete as long as the level of inefficiency did not exceed the value of the Canadian tariff relief. It was inevitable that a certain level of inefficiency would be present in such production because minimum cost in automobile production is not possible unless the level of output is expanded well beyond the requirements of the Canadian market and the US market was closed by the US tariff. The government had, in effect, created a high level of antiprotection and offered partial relief from this antiprotection as an incentive for producers to establish a line of production which would inevitably be inefficient. The 1965 Automobile Agreement was created as a remedy for this situation.

The 1965 agreement established a state of conditional free trade in automobiles and parts which was flexible enough to allow US automobile producers to specialize on both sides of the border. The government simultaneously reduced the tariff on the end products and the level of antiprotection. As expected, this led to a growth of trade and increased Canadian efficiency through continental specialization and economies of scale (Beigie, 1970, chaps. 6, 7). This outcome is predicted by the simulation, but the simulation takes no account of economies of scale. It is implicit in the simulation results that the price distortion due to the tariff is sufficient to restrain the level of production of autos, trucks, and parts (51) below the level it would reach under free trade pricing even in the absence of economies of scale. Fifty per cent of the costs of the autos, trucks, and parts (51) producer group are used to purchase high cost goods from the import competing sector and another fourteen per cent of costs are used to purchase the output of the domestic sector! Under these circumstances one would expect that the reduced level of antiprotection and the shift in relative prices would be effective in inducing expansion.

CONCLUSIONS

In 1961 Canada exported forty-four per cent of its iron ore (92) production. This is an indication of the amount of this resource which is processed outside of Canada and explains the Canadian desire to increase its share of production near the final stage of manufacturing. The tariff schedule is designed with the objective of encouraging such processing in Canada, but the simulation indicates that this has not been achieved under the pre-Kennedy tariff. All four end product classifications would expand under free trade. The situation is complex, but it is possible to identify certain characteristics which might help to clarify matters.

1. According to the simulation, the iron and steel sector is, as a whole, relatively repressed by the tariff schedules of Canada and the US. Even though the level of tariff protection escalates with the degree of processing, it has not succeeded in increasing the level of processing in Canada. Under free trade there would be a shift away from the later stages of processing of intermediate goods toward end product producer categories. Output of aircraft, autos, trucks,

buses, locomotives and transport equipment would be favoured if present levels of antiprotection could be reduced.

2. One of the more important causes of antiprotection in the iron and steel sector are the tariffs which apply to the large import competing classification (48). These intermediate product producers are important suppliers to other classifications in the iron and steel sector and to many industrial groups outside the iron and steel sector — particularly the nonferrous metal products producers.

3. The US tariffs which apply to the domestic classification (13) of the iron and steel sector and the export classification (33) appear to have the greatest effect on Canadian production. There is evidence that economies of scale are possible in some of the export lines. The US tariffs which applied to the domestic group (13) were higher than those that applied to the export classification (33).

4. The 'class and kind' clause which applies a higher rate of tariff to machinery and equipment (49) if produced in Canada increases costs of intermediate goods purchased for production in the end product classifications.

5. According to the simulation, output in the end product groups of this sector is less than warranted by comparative advantage. These are import competing classifications and hence sensitive to reductions in the Canadian tariff. Nevertheless, according to the simulation, many would expand in free trade. A reduction in direct protection without a simultaneous reduction in antiprotection would move these producers in a direction contrary to comparative advantage.

5

Non-ferrous metal, electrical, and other products

In this chapter, a broad spectrum of producer classifications is examined. In most, non-ferrous metal ores (90) are the principle resource content (other than labour and capital) but there are several exceptions. Gold and platinum ores (93) are the principle resource content of jewelry (61) and some classifications reveal no distinctive resource identity at all. As in the iron and steel sector, discussed in the previous chapter, we find that the Canadian-US tariff schedules shift the focus of production into the earlier stages of processing.

NON-FERROUS METAL PRODUCTS

Non-ferrous metal products is a classification sufficiently broad to include producers from the domestic, export, and import competing sectors of the economy. Consequently, in following the aggregation procedures described in chapter three it was necessary to establish three such producer categories. As may be verified with reference to Table 5.1, the ratio of trade to output must vary considerably between these groups. The ratio of trade to output in the domestic group (14) is 0.055, in the export group (34) it is 0.526, and in the import competing group (47) it is -0.187. Each of these is found to differ from the other two in the level of processing and in the resource content of output in a manner similar to that noted in connection with the iron and steel sector.

The domestic group (14) and the export group (34) specialize in intermediate goods which are produced at the earlier stages of processing. Output of producers in these two classifications consists largely of metals which have been cast, rolled, or extruded. The two groups differ in the type of metal used. The products of the domestic group (14) are made from tin, tin alloys, precious metals (excluding gold), and copper alloys, while in the export group (34) output is manufactured from nickel, copper, lead, or zinc. Output in the import

TABLE 5.1

Summary of data relating to value added and shipments of output from certain sectors to producers in the non-ferrous metal, electric, and other industries

Name of producer group	Value added (1)	Total Output (2)	Percentage intermediate shipments (3)	Ratio VA/TO (4)	Ratio Trade/TO (5)	Proportion of costs used to purchase[1]			
						D (6)	E (7)	M (8)	R (9)
14 Non-ferrous metal products, D	40,417	137,904	89.4	0.285	0.055	0.159	0.306	0.083	0.159
15 Electrical products, D	103,412	265,806	53.4	0.382	−0.037	0.119	0.202	0.289	0.001
16 Mineral products, D	180,294	408,716	98.6	0.421	0.019	0.263	0.155	0.054	0.087
34 Non-ferrous metal products, E	281,262	1,390,745	99.3	0.194	0.526	0.067	0.266	0.043	0.422
46 Graphite and carbon, M	10,268	26,290	99.2	0.381	−0.349	0.103	0.175	0.117	0.213
47 Non-ferrous metal products, M	266,622	689,249	87.5	0.378	−0.187	0.239	0.174	0.198	0.002
54 Electrical products, M	394,208	884,030	43.0	0.436	−0.367	0.193	0.065	0.294	0.002
55 Mineral products, M	129,824	267,229	82.2	0.472	−0.453	0.160	0.105	0.187	0.062
56 Petroleum products, M	271,649	1,254,962	58.7	0.210	−0.110	0.135	0.023	0.057	0.569
60 Scientific equipment, M	51,419	103,148	29.6	0.489	−0.850	0.177	0.091	0.231	0.003
61 Jewellery, M	40,842	85,680	18.9	0.470	−0.998	0.183	0.085	0.190	0.066
63 End products, NES M	131,199	286,434	38.4	0.448	−0.326	0.220	0.095	0.218	0.009

1 D refers to the domestic sector, E refers to the export sector, M refers to the import competing sector, and R refers to resource purchases.

TABLE 5.2

Summary of output and tariffs, taxes, and other data for the non-ferrous metal, electric, and other industries[1]

| Name of producer group | Taxes and government subsidies (1) | Transportation costs (2) | US tariff before Kennedy Round (3) | Canadian tariff | | Cost effect per dollar of TO | | Percentage change in output required to reach optimal level of production (8) |
				Before Kennedy Round (4)	After Kennedy Round (5)	Before Kennedy Round (6)	After Kennedy Round (7)	
14 Non-ferrous metal products, D	0.008	0.021	0.081	0.131	0.080	-0.001	-0.005	+0.52
15 Electrical products, D	0.007	0.023	0.140	0.136	0.099	-0.034	-0.033	+0.68
16 Mineral products, D	0.020	0.036	0.117	0.126	0.075	-0.009	-0.007	-0.04
34 Non-ferrous metal products, E	0.008	0.012	0.036	0.057	0.044	-0.003	-0.000	+0.02
46 Graphite and carbon, M	0.009	0.025	0.076	0.130	0.079	-0.011	-0.010	-10.00
47 Non-ferrous metal products, M	0.009	0.023	0.067	0.161	0.123	-0.020	-0.019	10.00
54 Electrical products, M	0.010	0.025	0.135	0.169	0.144	-0.037	-0.034	10.00
55 Mineral products, M	0.014	0.028	0.144	0.137	0.126	-0.018	-0.016	-0.10
56 Petroleum products, M	0.006	0.085	0.076	0.067	0.064	-0.006	-0.005	+0.01
60 Scientific equipment, M	0.009	0.022	0.211	0.091	0.086	-0.027	-0.025	10.00
61 Jewellery, M	0.007	0.021	0.158	0.142	0.120	-0.021	-0.021	+0.37
63 End products NES, M	0.010	0.029	0.140	0.197	0.163	-0.025	-0.022	-10.00

10 See note to Table 5.1.

TABLE 5.3

Shipments among industries in the non-ferrous metal, electric, and other industries[1]

Industry originating shipments	Industry receiving shipments											
	(14)	(15)	(16)	(34)	(46)	(47)	(54)	(55)	(56)	(60)	(61)	(63)
14 Non-ferrous metal products, D	0.014	0.001	0.007	0.007	0.005	0.006	0.006	0.000	0.002	0.013	0.064	0.010
15 Electrical products, D	0.000	0.007	0.000	0.000	0.000	0.000	0.015	0.000	0.000	0.002	0.001	0.001
16 Mineral products, D	0.001	0.000	0.109	0.000	0.000	0.001	0.000	0.006	0.000	0.001	0.001	0.001
34 Non-ferrous metal products, E	0.253	0.162	0.005	0.239	0.085	0.110	0.020	0.005	0.001	0.021	0.028	0.002
46 Graphite and carbon, M	0.004	0.000	0.000	0.010	0.008	0.000	0.003	0.000	0.000	0.001	0.002	0.000
47 Non-ferrous metal products, M	0.040	0.059	0.008	0.004	0.005	0.078	0.033	0.004	0.007	0.030	0.023	0.023
54 Electrical products, M	0.000	0.148	0.002	0.000	0.006	0.003	0.136	0.003	0.000	0.025	0.006	0.013
55 Mineral products, M	0.002	0.002	0.007	0.004	0.016	0.002	0.011	0.102	0.000	0.025	0.018	0.006
56 Petroleum products, M	0.006	0.002	0.018	0.011	0.020	0.003	0.002	0.018	0.011	0.002	0.001	0.005
60 Scientific equipment, M	0.000	0.000	0.000	0.000	0.000	0.000	0.001	0.001	0.000	0.001	0.000	0.000
61 Jewellery, M	0.004	0.000	0.000	0.000	0.000	0.000	0.001	0.000	0.000	0.044	0.075	0.002
63 End products, M	0.001	0.001	0.003	0.000	0.000	0.001	0.000	0.004	0.003	0.001	0.006	0.021
90 Metal ores, R	0.134	0.000	0.012	0.370	0.094	0.000	0.000	0.005	0.001	0.000	0.000	0.000

1 See note to Table 5.1.

competing group (47), on the other hand, consists of a large number of end products shipped to households and business firms. Culvert pipe, metal bottle caps, and coil springs are examples of such products.

Although the producers in both the domestic group (14) and the export group (34) are specialized at the earlier stages of processing, it appears that there are a greater number of producers at the early stages of processing in the export group (34). Producers in the export group (34) use a greater proportion of costs to purchase metal ores and use a greater proportion of costs to purchase resources in general. For the export group (34) purchases of metal ores (90) amount to thirty-seven per cent of cost while purchases of all resources amount to forty-two per cent of costs. The domestic group (14) uses only thirteen per cent of costs to purchase metal ores (90) and purchases from all resource groups amount to only sixteen per cent of cost.

Another indication of the processing hierarchy among these three groups is indicated by the magnitude of intermediate products shipped. The export group (34) is an important supplier to the other two non-ferrous metal products classifications but uses only one per cent of costs to purchase from these two classifications. Domestic producers are at the next higher stage of processing using twenty-five per cent of costs to purchase from the export group (34) and only 4 per cent of costs to purchase from the import competing group (47). The import competing group (47), itself, can be regarded as having the greatest number of end product producers. It uses none of its costs to purchase Metal Ores (90), and only 0.2 per cent to purchase resources. Eleven per cent of costs are used to purchase from the export classification which supplies metal ores indirectly (see Table 3.5 of chapter three).

The simulation indicates that all three classifications of non-ferrous metal producers would expand under free trade pricing but the greatest expansion occurs in the end product group which is import competing. This is by far the largest class of non-ferrous metal producers and the predicted expansion is the more remarkable because this is also the class where the weighted average Canadian tariff is the highest. The result is partly explained by the fact that the import competing group (47) purchases considerably more than the domestic and export groups from the domestic and import competing sector of the economy and is therefore relieved of a greater amount of antiprotection under free trade pricing.

Producers in the non-ferrous metals domestic and export groups purchase in greatest proportion from the export sector of the economy. The domestic group (14) uses thirty-one per cent of its costs to purchase from the export sector but only eight per cent of its costs are used to purchase from the import competing sector. Similarly the export group (34) uses twenty-seven per cent of its costs to purchase from the export sector of the economy but only four per cent of its costs to purchase from the import competing sector. Under free trade pricing the cost of goods purchased from the export sector rises relative to the cost of goods purchased from the domestic and import competing sector and this leaves producers in group (14) and group (34) worse off.

When the US tariff is reduced, producers in the export group (34) and some producers in the domestic group are encouraged to expand into the US market. The output of the export group (34), however, is concentrated on products at the early stages of processing and the US tariff on such items is very low. Consequently, the added incentive to expand is not great. Producers in the export (34) classification paid an average tariff of only 3.6 per cent pre-Kennedy. The US tariff applicable to the domestic group (14) was considerably higher, however, and could have been a critical factor limiting Canadian exports to 5.5 per cent of output.

All three non-ferrous metal product groups make significant purchases of iron and steel intermediate products. This can be confirmed if the reader will refer back to Tables 3.4 and 3.5 in chapter three which display the direct plus indirect resource content in each industry. The magnitude of these purchases is correlated with the degree of processing. Producers at the higher levels purchase the most. The export group (34), which is at the lowest level of processing, uses only one per cent of costs to purchase iron and steel intermediate products. The domestic group (14), on the other hand, which is one stage later in processing, uses ten per cent of costs to purchase intermediate iron and steel products. The import competing group (47), which is at the highest level of processing uses twenty-three per cent of its costs for such purchases. In chapter four we noted that there was a general dependence on iron and steel intermediate products in the end product classifications and argued that tariff reductions in the iron and steel intermediate products groups would shift the focus of production toward the end product stage.

Table 5.3 reveals the importance of the non-ferrous metals export group (34) as a supplier to other producers. The US tariff effectively creates a cost advantage to Canadian producers who purchase these exportable products and any further reductions in the US tariff will remove this advantage. The US tariff, applicable in the export group (34), is small and perhaps not of great significance. In free trade, therefore, the cost of intermediate goods supplied by the export group (34) will rise very little. Matters are somewhat different with regard to the output of the domestic producers in group 14. The US tariffs applicable to the domestic producers of non-ferrous metal products (14) may be preventing growth up to the level required by the simulation. The 1961 ratio of net exports to output indicates that some lines of production are exportable over an eight per cent US tariff and the simulation indicates that this is an area where output fell short of that required by the Canadian comparative advantage.

GRAPHITE AND CARBON

Graphite and carbon (46) is a small industry related to the non-ferrous metal products industries because of its purchases of metal ores (90). Nine per cent of costs are used for this purpose and from Table 3.5 of chapter three it can be verified that metal ores (90) also constitute fourteen per cent of the resource content of graphite and carbon (46) production. Since the ratio of net imports to output is –0.349, it is likely that in many lines of production the pre-Kennedy Canadian tariff was necessary to maintain the 1961 level of output. Nevertheless, the Kennedy Round reductions were comparatively large. The simulation indicates that, under free trade pricing, resources will be shifted out of Graphite and Carbon (46) production and into other activities.

This is an outcome that would be anticipated. Most of the direct tariff protection was needed and used in 1961. The loss of this protection is without offsetting reductions in the level of antiprotection. Producers of graphite and carbon (46) use only twelve per cent of costs to purchase intermediate products from the import competing sector of the economy and hence benefit very little from lower free trade prices. Expenditures in the export sector (where free trade prices tend to rise) are eighteen per cent of costs.

MINERAL PRODUCTS

It was necessary to establish only two classes of mineral products producers. Output of producers in the first class, group (16), consists of heavy products such as cement, lime, concrete basic forms, and bricks. These are shipped almost entirely to the domestic market. The ratio of net exports to output is only 0.019. This class of producers may be compared to group 55 which must be considered an import competing classification because the ratio of net imports to output is –0.435. In contrast to the heavy intermediate products of classification 16, the output of mineral products (55) consist of more highly processed items such as tableware, mineral wool, and glass tubing.

As far as purchases of intermediate products are concerned, the domestic and import competing groups have exactly opposite concentrations and, therefore, the indirect impact of the tariff schedule will also be in the opposite direction. Purchases of the domestic producer group (16) are concentrated on the export sector with lesser amounts purchased from the import competing sector of the economy. The import competing group (55) uses the greater portion of its costs to purchase from the import competing sector. Under a reduction in tariff levels, as in the Kennedy Round, the price of goods in the export sector of the economy rises relative to the price of goods in the import competing sector and this is a factor which should reduce the cost of producers in mineral products (55) relative to the domestic producers of group 16. During the Kennedy Round, the direct tariff reductions which applied to domestic producers in group 16 were considerably greater than the direct reductions which applied to the import competing producers of group 55. The import competing producers were favoured by a smaller reduction in tariff protection and also benefitted more from the general effect of the Kennedy Round on relative prices.

Nevertheless, this differential treatment probably had very little significance. Transport costs provide natural protection to the heavy products of the domestic group (16). Also, according to Table 5.1, Canada tends, if anything, to be a net exporter of these products. Consequently, we may assume that the pre-Kennedy Canadian tariff was, to some extent, redundant.

The level of production in the mineral products group does not seem to be influenced greatly by the Canadian resource base. Resources account for only nine per cent of the costs of group (16) and only six per cent of the costs of group (55). The import competing group (55) is not identified with any particular resource, but from Table 3.5 of chapter three one finds that the domestic producer group (16) accounts for almost all of the use of Canada's Sand and Gravel (102) and of her Stone (103). These resources are available in most areas of North America however[1] and consequently, transport costs to the market are more important in determining location than are resource supplies.

The simulation indicates that both mineral products groups will contract under free trade pricing. Although this conclusion holds on the average for both groups, it need not apply to every producer in these classifications. A partial equilibrium study by Wonnacott and Wonnacott (1967, 258), for example, led these authors to conclude that, with reorganization toward US standards of efficiency, the producers of asbestos products could become competitive with US producers. This conclusion is based on the assumption that a rather large amount of unexplained cost difference is due to diseconomies of small scale production and to other inefficiencies. In the simulation it is assumed that all firms are operating at maximum efficiency under constant returns to scale.

Producers of mineral products (55) supply intermediate goods to a long list of other producers. Nearly four per cent of the value of intermediate products required to produce liquor and beer (36) and eight per cent of the value of intermediate products required to produce alcohol and wine (39) are supplied by the import competing mineral products (55) group. According to the data of chapter nine expansion of both the liquor and beer (36) and alcohol and wine

(39) producers would be required for Canada to move closer to the optimal 1961 production pattern. The Canadian tariff applied to mineral products (55) explains, in part, the level of antiprotection present in these end product classifications.

ELECTRICAL PRODUCTS

It was necessary to establish a classification for electrical producers in both the domestic and the import competing sectors of the economy. Domestic producers are aggregated in group 15. Production is confined to television and radio receiving sets, radar equipment, and some wire production. The ratio of net imports to production in this group is only -0.037. The remaining electrical products producers are aggregated in the import competing group (54). These producers supply most of the major appliances such as washing machines, ranges, and vacuum cleaners, and a list of industrial products such as welding machinery and transformers. The ratio of net imports to production in these products is -0.367.

Both producer groups spend larger percentages of costs in the import competing sector of the economy than in the export sector. One might therefore assume that, under free trade pricing, the cost of intermediate goods would fall. According to the simulation, this decline in costs is sufficient to stimulate expansion under free trade pricing. The expansion is greatest in group (54) which purchases the greater amount from the import competing sector. If the level of antiprotection could be reduced either in group (15) or group (54), the expansion required in the simulation would be achieved without actually moving to free trade. The problem is complicated, however, by the interdependence of Canadian industries and the perverse effects of the Canadian tariff. Producers in the domestic group (15) use fifteen per cent of costs to purchase intermediate products from the import competing producers in classification (54). This latter group is itself subject to antiprotection. The domestic producers in group (15) use an additional twenty-two per cent of costs to purchase nonferrous metal products and, as noted above, non-ferrous metal products producers are, in turn, subject to antiprotection originating in the iron and steel intermediate products group. Both electrical groups produce a long list of durable consumer goods which cost perhaps twenty-five per cent more in Canada because of the inefficiencies generated by the Canadian tariff.

There has been a number of detailed cost studies of producers in the electric products classifications. Industries producing refrigerators, ranges and washing machines were studied by Eastman and Stykolt (1967, 231-54). This production is part of the output of the electric products (54) classification. The authors conclude from their study that none of the Canadian refrigerator or electric range production is carried on in plants of efficient size. Canadian production of refrigerators and ranges was inefficient compared to production in the US (Eastman and Stykolt, 1967, 250) and consumer prices for refrigerators were twenty-four per cent higher, and prices for ranges were twenty-eight per cent higher, in Canada than in the US (Eastman and Stykolt, 1967, 239). In a study of the electrical equipment producers, Wonnacott and Wonnacott (1967) obtain a similar result. The authors conclude (p. 258) that with free trade and greater specialization, this group could produce a limited range of commodities at costs low enough to become exportable to the US.

The average tariff applicable in the electrical products (15) domestic group was significantly reduced in the Kennedy Round while the tariff applicable to the import competing group (54) was only slightly reduced. In the case of domestic producers the change was probably of little effect because the tariff on domestic products tends to be above the level necessary for protection. The Canadian copyright law has been an additional avenue of protection for these pro-ducers in some cases.[2] The simulation implies that both producer groups would expand under free trade pricing but that the tariff on the final product cannot be reduced unless there are corresponding reductions in the level of antiprotection. The partial equilibrium studies cited above indicate that considerable gains could be achieved from further North American specialization, but complete removal of the Canadian and US tariffs would be a necessary condition for such an arrangement. This would not guarantee, however, that Canada would continue to maintain its present share of electrical production. The simulation, however, implies that a level of production at least as great, relatively, as the 1961 level is within the scope of the Canadian comparative advantage. Without corresponding reductions in antiprotection, however, free trade in electrical products would force some of the production at present located in Canada to shift to the United States. Because of the presence of economies of scale, this pattern could become irreversible.

PETROLEUM PRODUCTS

The 1961 output of the Petroleum Products (56) industry consisted principally of gasoline and fuel oil. Quantitatively, the output of such things as grease, butane, and asphalt was much less important. In no case did production of any minor product exceed ten per cent of the value of fuel oil. Fifty six per cent of the cost of producing Petroleum Products (56) is used to purchase Crude Oil (94). Crude Oil (94) is both imported and exported in large volume. The pattern of trade is determined by the location of oil reserves, the cost of recovering oil supplies, by transport costs (given the existing state of transport technology), and by public policy regarding the use and distribution of crude oil.

A notable feature of petroleum products (56) is the small percentage of costs used to purchase from either trade sector. Only 2.3 per cent of costs are used to purchase from the export sector and only 5.7 per cent of costs is used to purchase from the import competing sector. Only seven per cent of costs is spent on wages. Except for its importations of crude oil, the petroleum products (56) group is isolated from the remainder of the economy. The petroleum industry involves a large number of complicated issues that are outside the scope of this study. Under review are such matters as continental oil policy, new pipeline routes, the US and Canadian quota system with regard to crude oil, environmental questions, and the US and Canadian depletion allowances. Once decisions are made, substantial amounts of fixed capital are committed and it becomes costly to reverse policy. In such circumstances the tariff as such has only nuisance value.

OTHER END PRODUCTS

Scientific equipment (60), Jewelry (61), and end products NES (63) are classifications with only moderate connection to the other industries discussed in this chapter. The verbal titles describe the outputs of these industries as accurately as it is possible to do. It might, nevertheless, be helpful to provide some examples. Output of scientific equipment (60) includes measure, control, and aircraft nautical instruments. The output of the jewelry (61) group consists, in part, of watches, gem stones, and photographic equipment. End products NES (63) includes a host of small items such as brooms, bicycles, toys, needles, and phonograph records. In each case the output is of a type which does not enter further into production. Value added is nearly fifty per cent in all three groups and, in each, the percentage of costs used for wages is high.

Because the percentage of costs spent on the import competing sector exceeds the percentage spent on the export sector, the Canadian tariff raises the cost of intermediate goods by an amount equal to about two per cent. This is offset by a high Canadian tariff which probably raises the prices of Canadian goods by the full amount of the Canadian tariff. The ratio of net imports to output in the three end product groups is −0.850, −0.998 and −0.326 respectively for Scientific Equipment (60), Jewelry (61), and end products NES (63). Kennedy Round reductions were not large and, in the case of end products (63), the tariff is higher than its level in 1965 due to certain increases after 1965 but prior to the Kennedy Round.

The Canadian tariff is intended to favour production of goods at the later stages of processing relative to those at the earlier stages. It is questionable whether this is achieved in any way that can be measured objectively. The simulation indicates that, at free trade pricing, two of the three end product groups considered here would expand. Had Canada made most efficient use of her resources in 1961, these two groups would have been relatively larger. The tariff schedule has the effect of drawing too much of Canadian resources into production of intermediate products at the expense of end product groups. It is implicit in the simulation that the price of intermediate goods will fall under free trade relative to the prices of end products. The high levels of net protection in the end product groups is absolutely essential to the survival of these groups and yet it is not high enough to bring production up to the level that would be achieved at free trade pricing.

CONCLUSIONS

The tariff as it applies in the sector studied in this chapter has effects very similar to its effect in the iron and steel sector.

1. As in the iron and steel sector, the Canadian-US tariffs in the non-ferrous metal, electrical, and other products sectors has shifted the focus of production toward the earlier stages of processing. Under free trade pricing the end product categories scientific equipment (56), and jewellery (61) expand, but more significantly we note that, under the tariff, the earlier stages of intermediate processing are favoured relative to later stages in the non-ferrous metal products and electrical products classes.

2. The chain of cost escalation is well illustrated by the industries of this sector. Tariffs which protect iron and steel intermediate products are a noticeable cause of the antiprotection which is present in the non-ferrous metal products classifications and in mineral products (55). The direct protection in these latter classes escalates the antiprotection into the electrical products industries and other end product groups. Some of the output of the mineral products producers is an end product, but significant quantities of mineral products (55) are purchased by the alcohol and wine (39) and liquor and beer (36) producers who, therefore, in their turn, are affected by cost escalation.

3. Although the electrical products classes and the end product group (56) and group 63 would expand in free trade, Canada cannot eliminate the direct tariff protection until there is a reduction in the tariffs that apply at the earlier stages of processing. In the electrical products classifications there is evidence that economies of scale could be reached in some lines. If the level of antiprotection could be reduced in Canada and if the US tariff on these products could be eliminated, Canada would benefit from increased specialization in production. It has been observed that under present conditions Canadian consumers pay as much as twenty-five per cent more for electrical products.

4. The US tariff applying in the domestic classification of non-ferrous metal products (14) may be of greater significance than those which apply in the

export classification. There was a small flow of trade over the 1961 US tariff and this US tariff was higher than that prevailing in either the export or import competing classifications. Since the products of the domestic classification tend to be at a later stage of processing, the US tariff may be interpreted as preventing expansion at the later stage.

6

Wood and paper products

Canada's abundance of forest products gives Canadian producers in the wood and paper products sector a competitive advantage in the home market over firms located outside of Canada. In 1961 Canada was nearly self-sufficient in all of the wood and paper products classifications and exported almost seventy per cent of the wood pulp and paper (32). Printing (45) was the only classification of activities which faced substantial import competition. The wood products (12) and printing (45) classifications in this sector qualify as farthest along the line of processing. The mathematical simulation indicates that all would expand under conditions of free trade.

WOOD PRODUCTS PRODUCERS

In 1961 transport costs and a tariff of over twenty per cent were sufficient to keep the ratio of net imports to production of wood products (12) at -0.031. The magnitude of transport costs for the wood products (12) classification is indicated in column 2 of Table 6.2. Compared to other classifications in this study, the amount shown is quite large. Transportation adds to the costs of foreign producers selling in the Canadian market and this provides a source of competitive advantage to local producers in addition to the advantage created by the Canadian tariff. The output of this industry is considerably varied, however, and the effects of transportation costs will be of greater importance in some lines of production than in others. Furniture production is the largest single subclass in the wood products (12) classification and it is likely that for many of the products in this group, the ratio of value to weight is low which, accordingly, increases the amount of protection to the local producer.

    The relative abundance of forest resources in Canada is a factor which confers an advantage to local wood products (12) producers but this advantage does not

TABLE 6.1

Summary of data relating to value added and shipments of output from certain sectors to producers in the wood and paper sector

Name of producer group	Value added (1)	Total output (2)	Percentage inter-mediate ship-ments (3)	Ratio VA/TO (4)	Ratio trade/ TO (5)	Proportion of costs used to purchase[1]			
						D (6)	E (7)	M (8)	R (9)
12 Wood products, D	280,431	676,434	44.8	0.405	-0.031	0.180	0.174	0.180	0.052
28 Paper products, D	367,174	937,429	88.2	0.378	-0.063	0.321	0.105	0.085	0.097
32 Wood, pulp, and paper, E	878,630	2,025,186	95.8	0.421	0.682	0.109	0.140	0.039	0.279
45 Printing, M	321,292	586,076	57.3	0.536	-0.212	0.191	0.159	0.101	0.000

1 D refers to the domestic sector, E refers to the export sector, M refers to the import competing sector, and R refers to resource purchases.

TABLE 6.2

Summary of output and tariff and other data for the wood and paper sector[1]

Name of producer group	Taxes and government subsidies (1)	Transportation costs (2)	US tariff before Kennedy Round (3)	Canadian tariff		Cost effect per dollar of TO		Percentage change in output required to reach optimal level of production (8)
				Before Kennedy Round (4)	After Kennedy Round (5)	Before Kennedy Round (6)	After Kennedy Round (7)	
12 Wood products, D	0.009	0.051	0.116	0.204	0.160	−0.024	−0.022	+0.06
28 Paper products, D	0.014	0.023	0.098	0.162	0.140	−0.011	−0.009	+0.05
32 Wood, pulp, and paper, E	0.012	0.024	0.022	0.076	0.049	−0.004	−0.004	+0.03
45 Printing, M	0.012	0.011	0.081	0.122	0.113	−0.011	−0.008	+10.0

1 See note to Table 6.1.

TABLE 6.3

Shipments among industries in the wood and paper sector[1]

Industry originating shipments	Industry receiving shipments			
	(12)	(28)	(32)	(45)
12 Wood products, D	0.042	0.005	0.008	0.000
28 Paper products, D	0.015	0.223	0.013	0.072
32 Wood, pulp, and paper, E	0.117	0.036	0.059	0.112
45 Printing, M	0.000	0.007	0.000	0.071
84 Logs and bolts, R	0.044	0.001	0.135	0.000
86 Pulpwood, R	0.001	0.084	0.129	0.000

1 See note to Table 6.1.

accrue directly. Only five per cent of costs are used to purchase resources. These expenditures are used almost entirely to purchase logs and bolts (84). Resources are supplied indirectly through processed commodities purchased from the wood pulp and paper (32) classification. Canadian supplies of logs and bolts (84) can be exported to the United States over a very small (average 2.2 per cent *ad valorem*) tariff and, therefore, except for transport cost, the price advantage to Canadian producers is quite small.

The level of anti-protection in the wood products (12) producer group measures the extra cost per dollar of output of intermediate goods due to the impact of the Canadian tariff schedule. Even though Canadian producers of wood products (12) spend nearly equal amounts in the export and import sectors, the level of antiprotection is higher in this classification than in any other in the wood and paper sector. Goods purchased from the export sector are cheaper in Canada because the United States tariff raises the price in the US but the higher cost of goods purchased from the import competing sector are enough higher due to the Canadian tariff to generate -2.4 per cent anti-protection in the pre-Kennedy period. This is offset by the lower wages paid by Canadian firms. Wages account for thirty-one per cent of costs and, according to Wonnacott and Wonnacott (1967, 31) data wages paid by producers of wood products have in the past been relatively and absolutely lower in Canada than in the United States.

Greater detail about the costs of firms in the furniture industry is available from a study by Bond and Wonnacott (1968). Based on a survey of firms producing case goods and mattresses, the authors concluded that Canadian costs in furniture production generally exceed the US costs. The data indicated that seventeen per cent of this cost difference could not be explained by obvious items such as capital and materials costs. It was assumed that a substantial portion of the seventeen per cent reflected the inefficiency of small scale production in Canada. This analysis, however, is based on partial equilibrium assumptions. Exchange rates, wages, and prices were assumed constant in both Canada and the United States. The simulation described in chapter two of this study does not take Canadian wages, prices, or the exchange rates as fixed. The results of the simulation indicate that, at free trade prices, producers of wood products (12) would maintain or expand output relative to other producers even if economies of scale were not possible. If economies of scale are possible in part of this producer group, greater expansion would be expected.

The Bond and Wonnacott study cited above suggests that the performance of this group is not satisfactory, but to the extent that high transport costs are a barrier to trade we must assume that further reductions in the Canadian or US tariff are not likely to remedy the situation. Wood products (12) does not constitute a large percentage of purchases in any other producer classification and, therefore, does not generate antiprotection elsewhere in the economy by a significant amount. On the other hand, the simulation results indicate that the relative prices associated with the 1961 Canadian and US tariff levels were such as to prevent the wood products (12) producers from reaching the level of domestic output which would be expected under free trade pricing.

PAPER PRODUCTS

The amount of direct protection given to producers of paper products (28) is less than that allowed to producers of wood products (12) but the amount of protection less the amount of antiprotection is about the same in both groups. Furthermore, if we may judge from the ratio of imports to output, the paper products (28) producers face somewhat more import competition than the wood products (12) producers. Sales of both wood products (12) and paper products (28) are concentrated on the domestic market and it is therefore probable that the price is determined by domestic supply and demand within the range permitted by the tariff. In the case of paper products (28), however, the higher level of imports per unit of output implies that a greater proportion of the producers in this group make full use of the protection of the Canadian tariff. The tariff is lower in the case of paper products (28), but it may be closer to the critical point where import competition is essential.

Purchases of intermediate products by one member of the paper products (28) group from another are relatively high. In determining the classification system for this study, similar commodities were grouped together in a domestic category if both satisfied the criteria described in chapter 3, p. 67. The relatively large value of shipments from one member of paper products (28) to another indicates that several stages of processing are aggregated in the same classification. All stages are domestic and rely on the tariff to prevent foreign competition. Pricing, therefore, is determined by local conditions of supply and demand. Under these circumstances the tariff can operate as a shield for monopolistic pricing or inefficiency. If this is true for some of the members of this group, the higher prices become a form of antiprotection as far as the rest are concerned. This relationship is illustrated by two partial equilibrium cost studies which are available for two of the subsectors of paper products group.

The part of the paper products group devoted to production of container board has been studied in detail by Eastman and Stykolt (1967, 171-90). The authors found that, in the period of their study, ' ... prices for container-board in Canada were set collusively at levels higher than those that prevailed in the United States' (187). The performance of this industry was considered unsatisfactory with many suboptimal plants 'existing under the price umbrella held over them by major mills' (188). Also, the authors point out that in the post-war period, the adjustment of output to meet growing demand was slow, causing shortages which prevented expansion or created difficulties to producers of shipping containers. The unsatisfactory performance in Canada was aided by the Canadian tariff which prevented competition from outside Canada.

Eastman and Stykolt also studied the shipping container industry itself. Shipping containers are boxes made from corrugated container-board. In the case of container manufacturers, the authors concluded that regional markets were generally over-crowded with suboptimal firms. Nevertheless, prices were higher than could be explained by cost differences. Exceptionally high profits of thirty-four to fifty-five per cent were in evidence in 1948-54.

More recently we have a study by Haviland, Takacsy, and Cape (1968). The producers studied are the subset of paper products (28) which the authors describe as the Canadian pulp and paper industry excluding products manufactured from paper or paperboard. The conclusions of this study are guarded and pessimistic in tone but more optimistic than would be justified by our simulation. Based on a considerable amount of detailed information they conclude that, with re-organization of both production and marketing and with appropriate public policies, the part of the industry which they examined could become competitive in both the domestic and export markets but that the sector of the industry which is diversified and oriented to the domestic market could not succeed in North American markets against US competition.

In a study of the wrapping paper subgroup of paper products (28), Wonnacott and Wonnacott (1967, 259) are more pessimistic. They conclude that

Canadian producers operate under such extreme cost disadvantage that they could not survive even with reorganization.

Producers of paper products (28) are very much isolated from international competition. Relatively small amounts are purchased from either the export or import competing sectors. Most of the cost expenditure is used to purchase from other domestic producers or to make purchases of resource commodities — especially pulpwood (86). About two-thirds of domestic purchases are purchased by one member of the paper products (28) group from another member. The level of antiprotection is correspondingly low but in making the calculation of antiprotection we do not take account of the higher cost of the intermediate purchases within this group. Because of the Canadian tariff these will be higher in Canada by an amount that will be greater the greater the inefficiency of Canadian production and the greater the amount of oligopolistic pricing.

Kennedy Round tariff reductions in the paper products (28) group were relatively small. The evidence suggests that there is need for greater contact with foreign competition. This could be achieved by increased specialization and trade in North America if the Canadian-US tariffs were eliminated. The simulation implies that, on the average, producers of paper products (28) would expand under free trade pricing. This result is based on an analysis which neither takes economies of scale into account nor allows for improved performance through increased efficiency. Partial equilibrium studies suggest that improvement in both respects is possible in some of the activities of these producers. In certain cases there has been evidence of monopolistic pricing. Because of the large amount of internal cost dependence among paper products (28) producers, high pricing anywhere within the group reduces the competitiveness of all members.

WOOD PULP AND PAPER PRODUCERS

The wood pulp and paper (32) producers are important suppliers to all three of the other producer groups in the wood and paper sector. This may be verified by referring to Table 6.3. Output consists of intermediate products such as lumber, timber, railway ties and newsprint. Normally the lower cost home product would give firms using these as intermediate goods an advantage over their US competitors. Canada exports 68.2 per cent of its production and it may be safely assumed, therefore, that the Canadian tariff is of comparatively little importance. The US tariff, on the other hand, increases the cost of intermediate products purchased by US firms but the level of the US tariff was only 2.2 per cent in the pre-Kennedy period. As noted above, the low level of the US tariff diminishes the advantage of the Canadian location. On the other hand, evidence indicates that transportation costs may be important for firms in the wood consuming industries (Wonnacott and Wonnacott, 1967, 106), and this would give Canadian end product producers an advantage in the local market. Because of the Canadian resource base, large supplies of wood, pulp, and paper (32) can be made available at costs which do not exceed costs outside Canada.

Twenty-eight per cent of the costs of the wood, pulp, and paper (32) producers is used to purchase resources. Whether measured by value added or by total output these producers constitute a large group and play an important role in resource absorption. A large part of resource absorption consists of consumption of pulpwood (86), and the large Canadian production of this resource gives the Canadian producers of wood, pulp and paper (32) a natural advantage. On the other hand, here also the US tariff is low and presents no obstacle to a producer of wood, pulp, and paper (32) located in the US. At stages closest to resource production, the US tariff is low in order to minimize the processing advantage that is present in the nation where resources are produced.

The cost position of producers of wood, pulp, and paper (32) cannot be much affected by the nearly negligible amount of antiprotection present. Only four per cent of costs are used to purchase goods from the import competing sector. Producers of wood, pulp, and paper (32) benefit from the lower prices in Canada's export sector which accounts for fourteen per cent of costs. The simulation indicates that the level of wood, pulp, and paper (32) production would remain the same or increase under free trade pricing but the tariff schedules of Canada and the US have very little direct effect on costs.

A subgroup of the Wood, Pulp and Paper (32) producers has been studied in detail by Wonnacott and Wonnacott (1967, 258). The authors conclude that, if they were reorganized and had access to the US market, veneer and plywood producers would enjoy a free trade advantage of about three per cent over US producers under conditions of free trade. This conclusion is in agreement with the implications of the simulation.

CANADIAN PRINTING ACTIVITIES

The simulation indicates that, at free trade prices, the Canadian Printing (45) industry would have a cost advantage. The ten per cent expansion shown in column 8 of Table 6.2 is the maximum allowed by the linear programming algorithm. The ratio of imports to production in the pre-Kennedy period was twenty-one per cent. These imports were landed in spite of an average Canadian tariff of twelve per cent.

The Canadian advantage in printing derives from its indirect connection to the Canadian resource base. Direct purchases of resources are virtually nil, but a significant amount of cost is used to purchase paper products (28), and wood, pulp and paper (32). Both of these producer groups make substantial direct and indirect purchases of resources.

Part of the reason for the high proportion of printing imports can be found in the US copyright law. Until recently the US derived greater benefit from reciprocal copyright arrangements than did Canada. US printers had the advantage that more books are written by US authors than by Canadian authors, and books tend to be printed where they are written. Furthermore, a clause of the US copyright law withheld copyright protection from a book written by a US author if more than 1500 copies of the book were printed outside the US, and imported for sale on the domestic market.[1] Canadian imports of books and periodicals were twenty times the level of exports in 1964. Imports of miscellaneous items such as labels and tapes were a much smaller proportion of output. But even here, economies of scale work against the Canadian advantage. In cases where the Canadian firm is foreign owned the printing will be done in the foreign nation at costs which fully exploit economies of scale which can be realized from longer production runs.

Considerable reductions in the US tariff were achieved during the Kennedy Round. In the end, Canadian tariffs remained higher than US tariffs. It is unlikely that the US will consider further reductions without some concessions from Canada. Nevertheless, considering that expanded output in printing would move Canada toward its comparative advantage it would be in the interest of both nations if Canada had greater access to the US market. Most books already enter Canada duty free, but novels and books of fiction must pay a duty. A very large volume of miscellaneous printing also enters Canada duty free because the Canadian government assesses bulk shipments piece by piece and no single piece has a value greater than the one dollar minimum value for duty. An entire bulk shipment can, therefore, enter Canada duty free.

In exchange for eliminating the duty on novels and works of fiction, Canada might seek reductions in the US duty on miscellaneous printing. If the US tariff were eliminated entirely this would reduce the uncertainties of customs administration for Canadian printers who should be able to penetrate the US market. Expansion of this type would be along the lines of the Canadian comparative advantage yet allow both nations fully to exploit economies of scale. Low US tariffs on miscellaneous printing are in the interest of Canada but reductions in Canadian tariffs on books is in the interest of the US. The volume of books entering Canada in 1964 was seven times as great in value as imports of miscellaneous publishing. The value of output of miscellaneous publishing in Canada, on the other hand, exceeds the value of books published by a factor of four or five.

CONCLUSION

The simulation indicates that, under free trade pricing, 1961 output would have been relatively greater in all classifications in this sector. The Canadian-US tariff has the effect of reducing production at all the stages of processing.

The paper products (28) producer group is notable for the large proportion of purchases made between firms within the classification. The tariff protects members of this group and allows them to price above the US price by an amount equal to the US price plus the Canadian tariff. The Canadian tariff therefore becomes a factor which discourages producers from looking for lower cost intermediate products outside Canada. The higher cost of intermediate goods inflates the costs of firms which would otherwise demonstrate greater competitiveness and it encourages lines of production in Canada that cannot become competitive under any circumstances. Kennedy Round reductions in the Canadian tariff were relatively small. In the longer run, the evidence suggests that a more competitive environment is needed and that, in order for these producers to fully realize opportunities for large scale production, reductions in the US tariff are required. If by this means the cost of paper products (28) should be reduced it would reduce the level of antiprotection in printing (45).

Printing (45) is an area where Canadian production was below the optimal level. Because of economies of scale and the US copyright law, production of books in the past has been concentrated in the US. Canada has greater prospects for expanding her share of miscellaneous publishing than for expanding her share of book publishing. A reduction in the US tariff applicable to miscellaneous printed matter would open opportunities for Canadian producers to achieve production on a scale that would be competitive in the US. United States publishers have benefitted in the past from nearly free access to the Canadian market for books.

The simulation indicates that an increase in production of wood products (12) is in line with Canada's comparative advantage. This group has the disadvantage of a level of anti-protection which is higher than in any other producer group in the wood and paper sector and the Kennedy Round reductions were comparatively large. The largest subgroup in the wood products (12) classification is furniture which is an end product producer and which, therefore, generates very little antiprotection elsewhere in the economy. Evidence cited above indicates that there may be considerable inefficiency in the Canadian furniture industry due to the failure of firms to take full advantage of economies of scale.

7

Chemical and
chemical related industries

The aggregated value of output in the chemical industries is smaller than that of any other sector in this study. These producer groups are almost entirely domestic or import competing, and show only moderate cost relationship to the Canadian resource base. We may say, however, that the domestic and export sector, classifications (18) and (35) use considerably more non-metallic minerals (101) and more crude oil (94) and coal (96) purchases per dollar of output than is true in the import competing classifications 58 and 59. In this chapter these chemical producers are examined along with four other groups which have cost structures closely related to chemicals.

The classification system adopted for chemicals is the result, in part, of the aggregation rules described in chapter 3, p. 58. Chemicals (18) is the domestic classification in the chemicals sector. By selectively choosing the content of this class it was possible to obtain a producer group in which the ratio of net exports to output was only 0.025. Chemicals (58) and industrial chemicals (59) are the import competing classifications. The ratios of net imports to production in these groups are -0.263 and -0.148 respectively. In the group producing exportable chemicals almost all the output consists of inorganic chemicals and we therefore refer to this group as inorganic chemicals (35). The distinction between inorganic and industrial chemicals is to some extent arbitrary and the reader interested in the detailed content of this or any other classification is referred to Table 3.1 of chapter three for a more exact description. The ratio of net exports to output in the inorganic chemicals (35) group is 0.186.

EXPORTABLE CHEMICALS

Because nearly one-fifth of output is exported, one would expect that production in the inorganic chemicals (35) classification would expand under free trade pricing. The US tariff would be eliminated and the US price would initially be higher than the Canadian price. Production would need to increase in order to meet a higher level of demand for export. The simulation indicates that this would happen. Output of Inorganic Chemicals (35) would be relatively higher under free trade pricing.

It should be noted, however, that the US tariff on inorganic chemicals (35) is the lowest of all groups in the chemicals sector and the gains obtained when it is reduced are correspondingly small. Similarly, free trade brings very little relief from antiprotection. Purchases of intermediate goods are much more concentrated in the export sector of the economy and the per cent of costs spent in the import competing sector is small. Nevertheless, after adjustments in Canadian relative prices, the costs of Inorganic Chemicals (35) fall relative to other groups in this sector and consequently, these producers become more competitive.

IMPORT COMPETING CHEMICALS

In the import competing sector of the economy it is the Canadian tariff rather than the US tariff which is most influential. Because of the substantial flow of imports, one expects that costs are higher in Canada and that, therefore, Canadian prices of chemicals in groups (58) and (59) will be higher in many lines than prices in the United States by the amount of the Canadian tariff. The simulation indicates that the chemicals (58) and (59) classifications would contract relatively under free trade pricing.

It is interesting that a unilateral reduction in the Canadian tariff would favour the chemicals (58) group. The reduced cost of intermediate goods offsets the loss of direct protection. This is explained, in part, by the large percentages of cost in the chemicals (58) group which are used to purchase intermediate goods from the import competing sector of the economy relative to expenditures in the export sector. Also, expenditures in the domestic sector are relatively large and the cost of these commodities may also decline under free trade pricing. The cost situation with regard to industrial chemicals (59) is not unlike this, but to a lesser extent. Somewhat greater amounts are spent in the export sector and lesser amounts in the domestic and import competing sectors. However, a unilateral reduction of the Canadian tariff leads to contraction as in the case of free trade.

The data of Table 7.3 indicate that there is a considerable amount of cost interdependence in the chemicals sector. Under these circumstances conclusions obtained from partial equilibrium analysis are particularly suspect. The effect of tariff changes in any particular producer group depends on the cost and price

TABLE 7.1

Summary of data relating to value added and shipments of output from certain sectors to producers in the chemical sector

Name of producer group	Value added (1)	Total output (2)	Percentage intermediate shipments (3)	Ratio VA/TO (4)	Ratio trade/TO (5)	Proportion of costs used to purchase[1] D (6)	E (7)	M (8)	R (9)
17 Explosives, D	28,140	58,917	70.8	0.469	−0.020	0.258	0.105	0.149	0.011
18 Chemicals, D	45,433	93,983	85.1	0.466	0.025	0.171	0.107	0.180	0.060
19 Dressing and dyeing, D	14,111	24,872	100.0	0.557	0.000	0.143	0.094	0.189	0.008
35 Inorganic chemicals, E	92,232	219,266	95.1	0.404	0.186	0.165	0.224	0.126	0.065
57 Pharmaceuticals, M	111,642	295,095	29.0	0.367	−0.134	0.325	0.067	0.220	0.009
58 Chemicals, M	210,411	543,773	83.0	0.375	−0.263	0.224	0.081	0.266	0.042
59 Industrial chemicals, M	113,699	245,097	86.9	0.450	−0.148	0.169	0.092	0.244	0.032
62 Plastic products, M	43,918	115,822	77.9	0.369	−0.375	0.184	0.061	0.359	0.018

1 D refers to the domestic sector, E refers to the export sector, M refers to the import competing sector, and R refers to resource purchases.

TABLE 7.2

Summary of tariffs, taxes, and other data for the chemical sector[1]

| Name of producer group | Taxes and government subsidies (1) | Transportation costs (2) | US tariff before Kennedy Round (3) | Canadian tariff | | Cost effect per dollar of TO | | Percentage change in output required to reach optimal level of production (8) |
				Before Kennedy Round (4)	After Kennedy Round (5)	Before Kennedy Round (6)	After Kennedy Round (7)	
17 Explosives, D	0.009	0.023	0.188	0.099	0.095	-0.016	-0.014	-0.06
18 Chemicals, D	0.018	0.032	0.146	0.084	0.083	-0.021	-0.017	-2.18
19 Dressing and dyeing, D	0.011	0.024	0.000	0.000	0.000	-0.023	-0.019	-9.16
35 Inorganic chemicals, E	0.017	0.028	0.043	0.046	0.041	-0.010	-0.009	+5.53
57 Pharmaceuticals, M	0.011	0.028	0.072	0.159	0.099	-0.024	-0.023	-10.0
58 Chemicals, M	0.012	0.030	0.115	0.125	0.114	-0.034	-0.028	-2.06
59 Industrial chemicals, M	0.014	0.032	0.064	0.109	0.086	-0.028	-0.023	-10.0
62 Plastic products, M	0.010	0.023	0.172	0.122	0.141	-0.042	-0.034	+10.00

1 See note to Table 7.1.

TABLE 7.3

Shipments among industries in the chemical sector, 1961[1]

Industry originating shipments	Industry receiving shipments							
	(17)	(18)	(19)	(35)	(57)	(58)	(59)	(62)
17 Explosives, D	0.113	0.000	0.000	0.001	0.000	0.001	0.000	0.000
18 Chemicals, D	0.002	0.030	0.006	0.025	0.004	0.030	0.024	0.007
19 Dressing and dyeing, D	0.000	0.000	0.000	0.000	0.000	0.000	0.000	0.000
35 Inorganic chemicals, E	0.027	0.027	0.001	0.134	0.021	0.013	0.022	0.002
57 Pharmaceuticals, M	0.000	0.003	0.008	0.002	0.032	0.002	0.002	0.000
58 Chemicals, M	0.075	0.061	0.094	0.044	0.037	0.127	0.092	0.263
59 Industrial chemicals, M	0.018	0.020	0.015	0.012	0.026	0.029	0.043	0.015
62 Plastic products, M	0.005	0.001	0.010	0.000	0.015	0.006	0.003	0.011

1 See note to Table 7.1.

changes in all others. Lines of production which are most profitable after a tariff reduction utilize the resources and productive capacity previously employed by producer groups which are no longer competitive and there may be significant changes in demand for intermediate products. In a detailed assessment of the Canadian synthetic resins production, for example, Wonnacott and Wonnacott (1967, 259) concluded that Canada has an absolute cost disadvantage in this production. These producers are among the members of the import competing chemicals (58) group which contracts under free trade but expands if the Canadian tariff is reduced unilaterally.

PHARMACEUTICALS

Pharmaceuticals (57) is an end product group concentrating production on medical products, soaps, detergents, and other cleaning and scouring preparations. The pre-Kennedy tariff of sixteen per cent is comparatively large but, because of product differentiation, this is of lesser significance in the case of some producers in the pharmaceuticals (57) classification than it is in the case of producers in other classifications. Seventeen per cent of the costs of the pharmaceutical (57) producer group are used to purchase from members of the advertising and travel (27) classification. It must be assumed, therefore, that even though imports are thirteen per cent of output, the differential between the US and Canadian price will not be strictly established by the Canadian tariff. Over-all purchases are concentrated in the import competing sector of the economy which accounts for 22.0 per cent of costs. Total purchases from the export sector require only 6.7 per cent of costs. The Canadian tariff raises the costs of intermediate goods by 2.4 per cent in the pre-Kennedy period. Net protection is 13.5 per cent in the pre-Kennedy period but falls to a level of 7.6 per cent after the Kennedy Round changes. The simulation indicates that the relative level of output of the pharmaceuticals (57) group would decline under free trade pricing.

Synthetic detergent producers are members of the pharmaceuticals (57) classification. A detailed study of these producers is reported by Eastman and Stykolt (1967) who found that the Canadian tariff, in this case, did not have its usual effect of encouraging high cost production through overcrowding. The Canadian domestic market was large enough to permit full use of the capacity of all producing units. The authors conclude (Eastman and Stykolt, 1967, 225), however, that the Canadian tariff enabled these firms to charge higher prices in Canada than in the United States. It may be concluded, therefore, on the basis of partial equilibrium information, that production at the 1961 rate could be continued in the absence of the protective tariff if Canadian manufacturing units are operated at US levels of efficiency and prepared to operate at lower profit margins.

Pharmaceuticals (57) is a small end product producer group generating very little antiprotection, but hampered by the higher costs in Canada of intermediate goods. The Canadian tariff reductions under the Kennedy Round were substantial.

PLASTIC PRODUCTS

The output of the plastic products (62) group includes such basic items as plastic film and plastic sheet as well as end products such as plastic containers and hose. Canadian output in 1961 was concentrated on production of film and sheet where total output exceeded all other products by a wide margin. This is a small producer group highly dependent on the import competing sector and, in particular, on the chemical producer groups themselves. Nearly thirty-six per cent of costs is used to make purchases from the import competing sector while only six per cent of costs is used to purchase goods from the export sector. Total purchases from within the chemical sector require twenty-nine per cent of costs. Of this, twenty-eight per cent is used to purchase from the import competing portion of the chemical sector. Under these circumstances it is not surprising to find that the antiprotection of the Canadian tariff is very high. The costs of intermediate products purchased by plastic products are higher by 4.2 per cent in Canada due to the Canadian tariff. The apparent pre-Kennedy protection of 12.2 per cent therefore amounted to net protection of eight per cent.

The average tariff on plastic products (62) before the Kennedy Round, is lower than the average tariff after the Kennedy Round. The pre-Kennedy base year for this study is 1961. In the plastic products (62) group a number of tariff changes were made after 1965 but before the Kennedy Round. These changes had the effect of increasing the average tariff on plastic products (62) and the Kennedy Round reductions reduced the average tariff from this higher level leaving the average tariff on plastic products (62) after the Kennedy Round above the 1961 level. The 1961 level of the Canadian tariff was necessary to protect plastic products (62) producers but only because of the antiprotection generated by the Canadian tariff itself. Under free trade pricing relative prices would shift in favour of these producers and no tariff would be necessary.

DRESSING AND DYEING

Dressing and dyeing (19) is a set of activities offering services to the domestic textile producers. There were no recorded imports or exports in 1961. The dollar value of these activities is too small to affect significantly the costs of any of the textile industries and we have, therefore, classified them in the chemicals sector which is the most important supplier of intermediate goods. About twelve per cent of the purchases of dressing and dyeing (19) is used to purchase chemicals. Wages are the most important cost item in dressing and dyeing (19). Forty-seven per cent of costs is used for wages. Consequently, value added is also high, reaching 55.7 per cent of costs. The percentage of cost spent in the import competing sector exceeds the amount spent in the export sector. About nineteen per cent of costs is used in the import competing sector while only nine per cent is used to purchase goods from the export sector. The Canadian tariff on intermediate purchases raises the cost of goods purchased by Dressing and Dyeing (19) by 2.3 per cent in the pre-Kennedy period. The simulation indicates that these activities would contract under free trade pricing.

EXPLOSIVES

The output of explosives (17) is also quite small. Like the dressing and dyeing (19) activities, production of explosives is very labour intensive. The ratio of wages to total output is well above the other industries in the chemicals group and high compared to all other industries in this study. Costs tend to concentrate on the import competing sector but the excess of expenditures in the import competing sector over expenditures in the export sector was only five per cent. The amount that the cost of intermediate goods are raised by the Canadian tariff are offset by the relatively lower cost in Canada of goods purchased from the export sector. The antiprotection of the Canadian tariff was − 1.5 per cent. The simulation indicates that the relative size of this producer group would contract under free trade pricing.

CONCLUSIONS

The cost data of Table 7.3 indicate that the import competing producers of chemicals (58) play a key role as suppliers in the chemical sector. The simulation indicates that this group will contract in free trade but would expand if the Canadian tariff were reduced unilaterally. The changes recorded for other groups in the chemicals sector must be judged in comparison to this. Producer groups 17, 18 and 19 are small, and the changes required by the linear programming algorithm are small in percentage terms. The significant adjustment in the chemicals sector occur in groups 35, 57, 58, 59, and 62, all of which except the first form a part of the import competing sector.

At free trade pricing, inorganic chemicals (35) and plastic products (62) have the greatest prospects for expansion. Expansion can be encouraged by reductions in antiprotection and in the case of inorganic chemicals (35) by reductions in the US tariff. Chemicals (58) is an important supplier to the chemical groups which should expand to reach the relative level required by comparative advantage. A reduction in the Canadian tariff on chemicals (58) would encourage expansion of inorganic chemicals (35) and in plastic products (62). A reduction should also be made in net protection applying to chemicals (18) and chemicals (59) but these classifications are quantitatively less important as suppliers to other groups. We may infer from the large percentage of costs used to purchase the output of the export sector that the resource content of the inorganic chemicals (35) group is in line with relative resource abundance in Canada. The exporting producer group (35) and the domestic producers in chemicals (18) differ from the other producers of chemicals in that there is a notable direct plus indirect use of metal ores (90) and non-metallic minerals (101). The ratio of intermediate shipments to total output is exceptionally high in all of the chemistry classifications except pharmaceuticals (57) and it is therefore difficult to discuss the projected changes in terms of the processing hierarchy.

8

Textile products

A comparative advantage in textile production cannot be established in Canada on the basis of relative resource abundance. Neither raw cotton (64) nor rubber (65) is produced domestically and, although there is some production of wool in the grease (83), the total amount of this production was less than the amount imported in 1961. With the exception of leather (11) all textile producers face substantial import competition from the densely populated regions of the world which typically have a comparative advantage because of lower labour costs. Rather than competing with these nations in textile production, Canada might more successfully seek expansion in other lines where, by virtue of her natural endowment, she can produce competitively. The densely populated regions of the world are particularly in need of the products of Canadian agriculture and industry but such products cannot be purchased from Canada unless these areas have a means of earning Canadian dollars. In this chapter we examine the circumstances prevailing in the principle textile producing industries. Unlike the sectors studied in the previous chapters there is a clear-cut tendency in textiles for Canada to shift to earlier stages of processing under free trade pricing.

LEATHER AND LEATHER PRODUCTS

The textile sector has two classifications for leather. One of these, leather products (41), consists principally of producers of finished products such as shoes, handbags, and luggage. The other classification produces the intermediate product, leather (11). The raw material group is meat except fish and poultry (3). Forty-one per cent of the cost of leather (11) production is used to purchase hides which are a by-product of the meat except fish and poultry (3) group. An available supply of hides is obviously an important factor determining the location of leather production. Because of the high costs of handling and transport,

TABLE 8.1

Summary of data relating to value added and shipments of output from certain sectors to producers in the textile sector

Name of producer group	Value added (1)	Total output (2)	Percentage intermediate shipments (3)	Ratio VA/TO (4)	Ratio Trade/TO (5)	Proportion of costs used to purchase[1] D (6)	E (7)	M (8)	R (9)
11 Leather, D	14,653	56,648	99.7	0.249	0.037	0.560	0.071	0.102	0.009
40 Rubber products, M	134,600	306,971	68.4	0.428	−0.170	0.121	0.053	0.381	0.007
41 Leather products, M	90,287	225,075	7.9	0.395	−0.124	0.358	0.040	0.200	0.001
42 Cotton textile products, M	87,390	250,023	87.2	0.341	−0.561	0.095	0.044	0.507	0.004
43 Wool textile products, M	40,303	105,632	81.9	0.373	−0.529	0.087	0.066	0.415	0.050
44 Other textile products, M	607,118	1,597,479	32.7	0.373	−0.162	0.135	0.039	0.429	0.017

1 D refers to the domestic sector, E refers to the export sector, M refers to the import competing sector, and R refers to resource purchases.

TABLE 8.2

Summary of tariffs, taxes, and other data for the textile sector[1]

Name of producer group	Taxes and government subsidies (1)	Transportation costs (2)	US tariff before Kennedy Round (3)	Canadian tariff		Cost effect per dollar of TO		Percentage change in output required to reach optimal level of production (8)
				Before Kennedy Round (4)	After Kennedy Round (5)	Before Kennedy Round (6)	After Kennedy Round (7)	
11 Leather, D	0.010	0.111	0.075	0.152	0.134	-0.011	-0.009	-9.00
40 Rubber products, M	0.011	0.023	0.096	0.148	0.125	-0.052	-0.047	+10.0
41 Leather products, M	0.006	0.031	0.115	0.247	0.224	-0.040	-0.035	-10.0
42 Cotton textile products, M	0.009	0.020	0.131	0.217	0.192	-0.070	-0.058	-10.0
43 Wool textile products, M	0.008	0.027	0.330	0.247	0.210	-0.084	-0.073	+0.61
44 Other textile products, M	0.007	0.036	0.228	0.255	0.225	-0.073	-0.065	-9.39

1 See note to Table 8.1.

TABLE 8.3

Shipments among industries in the textile sector[1]

Industry originating shipments	Industry receiving shipments					
	(11)	(40)	(41)	(42)	(43)	(44)
11 Leather, D	0.001	0.002	0.206	0.000	0.000	0.003
40 Rubber products, M	0.000	0.025	0.046	0.003	0.000	0.003
41 Leather products, M	0.000	0.006	0.047	0.000	0.000	0.000
42 Cotton textile products, M	0.000	0.086	0.024	0.195	0.046	0.116
43 Wool textile products, M	0.000	0.006	0.006	0.007	0.223	0.051
44 Other textile products, M	0.000	0.016	0.015	0.096	0.093	0.212
64 Raw cotton, NCM[2]	0.000	0.001	0.000	0.174	0.018	0.003
65 Rubber, NCM	0.000	0.055	0.001	0.000	0.000	0.000
82 Fur, R	0.000	0.000	0.000	0.000	0.000	0.015
83 Wool in the Grease, R	0.000	0.000	0.000	0.000	0.046	0.000

1 See note to Table 8.1.
2 NCM refers to non-competing imports.

hides are usually processed to the stage of leather in the near vicinity of slaughter houses. The data of Table 8.2 indicate that eleven per cent of the cost of producing leather (11) is used to pay for transport costs.

At the leather products (41) stage, cost factors other than the cost of hides dominate the situation. Hides are incorporated in leather products (41) at the stage of processing where leather (11) is produced. Forty-one per cent of the value of leather (11) derives from the cost of purchasing hides but the output of leather (11) constitutes only 20.6 per cent of the cost of leather products (41). The cost of the hide content in leather products (41), therefore, is only eight per cent. This can be compared to some of the items of direct labour costs incurred in production of leather products (41). Thirty-seven per cent of costs are used for wages. The direct cost of purchases from the rubber products (40) group is about equal to the cost of hides. About five per cent of the cost of leather products (41) is used to purchase the output of rubber products (40). Therefore, at the end product stage the high transport cost in the earlier stages becomes comparatively insignificant and location is more determined by other factors which, in Canada, make it advantageous to export leather (11) and import leather products (41).

The simulation implies that the output levels of both leather (11) and leather products (41) would decline relatively under free trade pricing. This decline is the logical consequence of the decline in meat except fish and poultry (3) group discussed in chapter nine. Under free trade pricing the supply of hides will decline and hence the number converted to leather is decreased. If as a consequence of free trade Canada should increasingly specialize in production of live cattle with the United States specializing in meat production, the supply of hides will be further reduced and leather (11) production will be increasingly located in the United States. It does not follow that the United States will become the location for an expanded production of leather products (41). Both Canada and the United States export leather to lower wage nations such as Spain, Italy, Japan, and the UK. Leather products are imported from these nations and from Hong Kong. There are indications that this is a proper line for international specialization but the shift is bound to be resisted. In 1966, for example, the United States imposed an export quota on hides.

RUBBER AND RUBBER PRODUCTS

The tariff on raw rubber is not an important cost factor as far as production of rubber products (40) is concerned. Rubber can be imported duty free under several tariff items and the average tariff on imported raw rubber (65) is very low. The rubber products (40) group, as a whole, uses only 5.5 per cent of cost to purchase raw rubber (65). Purchase from the import competing sector of the economy, on the other hand, are relatively large. Thirty-eight per cent of costs is used to purchase intermediate goods from the import competing sector but only 5.3 per cent is used make purchases from the export sector. Purchases of cotton textile products (42) alone account for 8.6 per cent of costs and this exceeds the percentage of cost spent on raw rubber (65). Because so much of cost is used to make purchases from the import competing sector of the economy, the Canadian tariff raises cost in Canada five per cent above the cost of similar goods in the United States. This takes away nearly one-third of the nominal protection of this group. In the pre-Kennedy period the tariff in Canada was 14.8 per cent but net protection amounted to less than 10 per cent. In recent times the tariff protection has been supplemented by a system of voluntary export constraints under which some of the exporting nations agree to limit sales in Canada (see Stegeman, 1973, chap. 2).

The simulation indicates that an expanded output of rubber products (40) would be expected under free trade pricing and that a relative increase in the output of rubber products (40) is in line with Canada's comparative advantage. This conclusion is corroborated by a more detailed study of tire production. On the basis of a partial equilibrium cost study, Wonnacott and Wonnacott conclude (1967, 258) that Canadian production of tires could reach US standards of efficiency if reorganized and if Canadian producers had free entry to the US market. From the high percentage of rubber products (40) now imported into Canada we might conclude that this is not likely to apply to the sector as a whole. The simulation does suggest, however, that domestic output would expand under free trade pricing. The high level of antiprotection is a fundamental obstacle to this growth. Without compensation in the form of direct protection, it is likely that the output would fall. If we rule out increases in direct tariff protection, the incentive for expansion must come through reduced antiprotection.

COTTON TEXTILES

Cotton textile products (42) are outputs made almost entirely of cotton, usually at the earlier stages of processing. Cotton yarn, woven cotton, cotton thread, and bed sheets are typical output. Of the inputs, raw cotton (64) is the most important. Seventeen per cent of the costs of cotton textile products (42) is used to purchase raw cotton (64). End products of cotton are classified with other textile products (44) which are described in more detail below.

Although 17.4 per cent of the costs of cotton textile products (42) go to purchase raw cotton (64), the tariff on raw cotton (64) does not significantly affect costs. The average tariff on raw cotton (64) was only 2.5 per cent in the pre-Kennedy period and cotton not further manufactured than ginned could be imported duty free under tariff item 52005-1. Although the Canadian tariff does not raise resource prices, it does have a substantial effect on the cost of cotton textile products (42) indirectly, by increasing the prices of intermediate goods purchased from the import competing sector of the economy. Fifty-one per cent of the costs of cotton textile products (42) is used to purchase goods from the import competing sector as a whole but only 4.4 per cent of costs is used to purchase goods from the export sector.

Of the purchases made from the import competing sector of the economy a large part are made from firms in the textile sector itself. Twenty per cent of costs is used by members of the cotton textile products (42) group to purchase intermediate products from each other and ten per cent of costs is used to purchase intermediate products from producers in the other textile products (44) classification. The ratio of net imports to output in the cotton textile products (42) group is -0.561. We may therefore assume that most of the members of this group price up to the tariff. The average tariff for the group was 21.7 per cent before the Kennedy Round but there was an amount of anti-protection equal to seven per cent. Accordingly, net protection was reduced to 14.7 per cent.

WOOL TEXTILE PRODUCTS

Wool textile products (43) consist of outputs made almost entirely of wool, often at the earlier stages of processing. Wool yarn, woven yarn, woollen blankets, and carpet are examples of these products. End products partly of wool are classified with other textile products (44) which are discussed in the next section. With the exception of wool textile products (43), none of the industries in this study use wool in the grease (83). Although the entire Canadian production of wool in the grease (83) plus imports is used by the wool textile products (43) group, purchases of wool amount to only 4.6 per cent of costs. Like other groups producing textiles, costs are concentrated on purchases of intermediate goods from the import competing sector of the economy. Purchases from the import competing sector amount to 41.5 per cent of costs. Purchases from the export sector however, require only 6.6 per cent of costs. The average pre-Kennedy tariff of 24.7 per cent, applicable to the end product, is offset by the higher cost of intermediate goods purchased from the import competing sector. Anti-protection equal to -8.4 per cent of cost leaves the amount of net protection equal to 16.3 per cent pre-Kennedy.

These calculations are made on the basis of most favoured nation tariff rates. Most imports of wool textile products (43) come into Canada under the British preference rates which are about five to ten per cent lower than the most favoured nation rate. The difference is more than offset, however, by the higher shipping cost of goods from Europe. According to expert opinion on this point, eleven per cent is the average amount of cost of insurance and freight on Atlantic shipping (Committee for Economic Development, 1963, xiii).

OTHER TEXTILE PRODUCTS

It was intended that the activities of firms classified in the other textile products (44) group would consist of processing beyond the stages reached in the cotton textile products (42) and wool textile products (43) classifications. Output includes end product items such as shoe laces, awnings, curtains, hosiery, and rain coats. Direct purchases of resource commodities are negligible but purchases of intermediate products from the cotton textile products (42) and wool textile products (43) classifications are substantial. There is considerable inter-dependence of costs in the textile sector. Producers in the intermediate cotton textile products (42) classification use ten per cent of costs to purchase other textile products (44), and producers in the intermediate wool textile products (43) classification use nine per cent of cost for such purposes. Furthermore, producers in all three classifications make substantial purchases from other producers within the same classification.

The US tariff has very little effect on the prices or costs of producers in the other textile products (44) classification. The intermediate goods purchased from the other textile products (44) group come primarily from the import competing sector where prices are governed by the Canadian tariff. The import competing sector accounts for forty-three per cent of costs while purchases of intermediate goods from the export sector of the economy amount to only four per cent. Consequently, there is an amount of antiprotection equal to -7.3 per cent of costs. The Canadian average tariff for this group of producers was 25.5 per cent. Since the ratio of net imports to output is -0.162, it is likely that output prices in Canada exceed prices in the US in many lines by the full amount of the Canadian tariff. Net protection, pre-Kennedy, is eighteen per cent.

The simulation indicates that the level of output in the other textile products (44) classification was too high in 1961 relative to other groups in this sector and that the textile sector would be more competitive if resources were shifted to other lines of production. The implicit decline in the output of other textile products (44) applies to the classification as a whole under free trade pricing but does not necessarily apply to each individual activity in the group. There is a large variety of commodities produced by the members of this classification, and since the output consists of many end products, market proximity is important. In a detailed study of cost structure in the men's clothing industry, for example,

Wonnacott and Wonnacott (1967, 258) concluded that, with reorganization and free trade, the men's clothing industry could successfully compete in free trade, but they emphasized that this could be true only if these producers have access to intermediate goods at prices available to firms located in the United States.

GENERAL ASPECTS OF THE TEXTILE SECTOR

There is no evidence to suggest that Canada has a comparative advantage in production of textiles. The large flows of imports over relatively high tariffs imply that the present levels of output are maintained at very high cost to the economy as a whole. The output of the textile sector is an important item in the budget of lower income consumers. The government must decide whether it is wise to add twenty-five per cent to prices of textiles for the purpose of expanding the relative size of this low wage sector. As long as present levels of protection exist, business firms will find it profitable to invest in the textile sector and there will be a lesser amount of investment in lines of production where Canada has a comparative advantage.

The US tariff is of very little significance as far as Canada is concerned. The high levels of price distortion are entirely due to the Canadian tariff. The data of Table 8.3 demonstrate that there is considerable cost interdependence among producers in the textile sector. In reviewing these data the value of goods shipped from the cotton textile products (42) group and the wool textile products (43) group should be considred in terms of the size of these classifications. Although the cotton textile products (42) group is only one-sixth as large as the other textile products (44) classification, it provides twelve per cent of the intermediate products required by this latter group. The tariff which applies to the relatively small cotton textile products (42) classification generates an amount of antiprotection in the other textile products (44) producer group that is out of proportion to size. The simulation indicates that the tariff has had the effect of expanding the output of other textile products (44) and cotton textile products (42) relative to wool textile products (43), and rubber products (40).

The high levels of antiprotection characteristic of all industrial groups in the textile sector are its most notable feature. As a consequence, a higher level of direct protection is needed in each industry to achieve a given amount of net protection. If it is the objective of tariff negotiations to move the system in the direction of its free trade solution, this should proceed in stages with rates in the Other Textile Products (44) and cotton textile products (42) to be reduced first. This would reduce the level of antiprotection in rubber products (40) and wool textile products (43) classes and lead to reduced costs relative to prices of output in these groups.

9

Agriculture and food

Because it is the product of land, output in many classifications in the agriculture and food sector can be regarded as resource production, but in some cases it would also qualify as an end product because of the large percentage of output shipped directly to consumers. All nations, including Canada, protect agriculture production at the resource stage with tariff and non-tariff barriers. It is then necessary to protect later stages of processing as well. According to the simulation this policy succeeded in some cases but failed in others. There is no discernible relationship between protection and the degree of processing. The three largest intermediate product producing classifications operated at a higher level of processing with the tariff than would be the case in free trade.

RESOURCE DEPENDENT DOMESTIC INDUSTRIES

Meat except fish and poultry (3), processed poultry (4), dairy products (5), feed meal (6), and processed tobacco (10) are the domestic producer groups which use the greatest percentage of costs to purchase agricultural resources. This percentage ranges between thirty and fifty-five. (The exact percentage for particular producers is shown in Table 9.1). In each classification purchases are concentrated on one or two resources. These can be identified from Table 3.4 of chapter three. Forty-four per cent of the costs of the meat except fish and poultry (3) producers is used to purchase from live animals (71), and thirty-six per cent of the costs of the processed poultry (4) producers are used in this resource classification. The dairy products (5) classification uses fifty-four per cent of costs to purchase unprocessed milk (74), the processed tobacco (10) producers use thirty-one per cent of costs to purchase raw tobacco (81), and in the feed meal (6) classification ten per cent of costs is used to purchase wheat (72) and nineteen per cent to purchase other grains (73).

TABLE 9.1

Summary of data relating to value added trade and shipments of output from certain sectors to producers in the food and agriculture sector

Name of producer group	Value added (1)	Total Output (2)	Percentage intermediate shipments (3)	Ratio VA/TO (4)	Ratio trade/TO (5)	Proportion of costs used to purchase[1]			
						D (6)	E (7)	M (8)	R (9)
1 Services to agriculture, D	37,449	64,133	92.2	0.547	0.000	0.221	0.078	0.082	0.035
3 Meat except fish and poultry, D	326,648	1,377,636	29.1	0.230	0.000	0.228	0.047	0.043	0.445
4 Processed poultry, D	72,622	228,401	22.4	0.310	-0.025	0.255	0.040	0.022	0.364
5 Dairy products, D	191,805	895,229	20.9	0.204	-0.014	0.164	0.037	0.039	0.546
6 Feed meal, D	39,906	298,089	95.6	0.148	0.009	0.238	0.165	0.159	0.304
7 Cereal and bakery, D	101,844	251,737	12.5	0.389	-0.033	0.305	0.154	0.117	0.019
8 Sugar refinery products, D	38,649	131,853	55.4	0.285	-0.041	0.083	0.050	0.467	0.107
9 Confectionary products, D	47,690	142,893	0.7	0.325	-0.053	0.303	0.082	0.233	0.048
10 Processed tobacco, D	77,616	331,276	24.3	0.228	0.057	0.419	0.022	0.017	0.308
29 Fish products, E	40,020	182,626	40.1	0.213	0.575	0.127	0.113	0.047	0.493
30 Flour, Malt, and starch, E	131,447	481,550	39.6	0.261	0.149	0.206	0.141	0.107	0.274
31 Beet, pulp, and sugar, E	9604	24,084	52.4	0.378	0.248	0.221	0.081	0.232	0.067
36 Liquor and beer, E	199,681	408,791	8.7	0.466	0.091	0.227	0.152	0.099	0.033
38 Processed foods, M	283,816	924,948	32.9	0.296	-0.241	0.239	0.063	0.237	0.155
39 Alcohol and wine, M	9461	21,440	18.1	0.427	-0.432	0.173	0.069	0.182	0.136

1 D refers to the domestic sector, E refers to the export sector, M refers to the import competing sector, and R refers to resource purchases.

TABLE 9.2

Summary of tariffs, taxes, and other data for the food and agriculture sector[1]

Name of producer group	Taxes and government subsidies (1)	Transportation costs (2)	US tariff before Kennedy Round (3)	Canadian tariff		Cost effect per dollar of TO		Percentage change in output required to reach optimal level of production (8)
				Before Kennedy Round (4)	After Kennedy Round (5)	Before Kennedy Round (6)	After Kennedy Round (7)	
1 Services to agriculture, D	0.037	0.044	0.000	0.000	0.000	-0.010	-0.008	-0.04
3 Meat except fish and poultry, D	0.008	0.025	0.073	0.105	0.088	-0.005	-0.005	-0.28
4 Processed poultry, D	0.008	0.030	0.000	0.120	0.120	-0.003	-0.002	-0.19
5 Dairy products, D	0.011	0.013	0.081	0.148	0.145	-0.005	-0.004	-0.08
6 Feed meal, D	-0.014	0.051	0.049	0.111	0.068	-0.016	-0.019	-0.05
7 Cereal and bakery, D	0.015	0.034	0.031	0.143	0.114	-0.007	-0.010	-0.02
8 Sugar refinery products, D	0.008	0.029	0.121	0.185	0.182	-0.031	-0.008	-1.33
9 Confectionery products, D	0.009	0.031	0.109	0.203	0.169	-0.025	-0.024	+0.01
10 Processed tobacco, D	0.006	0.017	0.386	0.494	0.262	-0.003	-0.002	+0.01
29 Fish products, E	0.006	0.023	0.069	0.089	0.048	-0.004	-0.006	+0.03
30 Flour, malt, and starch, E	0.012	0.043	0.070	0.173	0.109	-0.007	-0.009	+0.54
31 Beet, pulp, and sugar, E	0.021	0.037	0.076	0.239	0.153	-0.019	-0.016	-10.0
36 Liquor and beer, E	0.023	0.021	0.146	0.441	0.073	-0.001	-0.004	+10.0
38 Processed foods, M	0.011	0.029	0.091	0.136	0.091	-0.040	-0.036	-5.65
39 Alchohol and wine, M	0.014	0.038	0.124	0.134	0.138	-0.021	-0.017	+10.0

1 See note to Table 9.1.

TABLE 9.3

Shipments among industries in the food and agriculture sector[1]

Industry originating shipments	Industry Receiving Shipment														
	(1)	(3)	(4)	(5)	(6)	(7)	(8)	(9)	(10)	(29)	(30)	(31)	(36)	(38)	(39)
1 Services to agriculture, D	0.019	0.000	0.001	0.000	0.000	0.000	0.000	0.000	0.000	0.000	0.000	0.009	0.000	0.000	0.000
3 Meat except fish and poultry, D	0.001	0.129	0.017	0.001	0.049	0.037	0.000	0.005	0.005	0.015	0.020	0.009	0.002	0.015	0.002
4 Processed poultry, D	0.000	0.001	0.111	0.000	0.000	0.001	0.000	0.000	0.000	0.000	0.001	0.001	0.000	0.007	0.000
5 Dairy products, D	0.000	0.001	0.001	0.065	0.004	0.010	0.000	0.025	0.000	0.000	0.007	0.004	0.000	0.009	0.000
6 Feed meal, D	0.081	0.003	0.003	0.001	0.072	0.001	0.000	0.000	0.000	0.000	0.002	0.037	0.000	0.000	0.000
7 Cereal and bakery, D	0.000	0.000	0.000	0.000	0.000	0.001	0.000	0.001	0.000	0.000	0.015	0.000	0.002	0.000	0.000
8 Sugar refinery products, D	0.000	0.001	0.000	0.004	0.007	0.034	0.000	0.053	0.002	0.000	0.001	0.009	0.002	0.034	0.009
9 Confectionery products, D	0.000	0.000	0.000	0.000	0.000	0.001	0.000	0.003	0.000	0.000	0.001	0.000	0.000	0.000	0.000
10 Processed tobacco, D	0.000	0.000	0.000	0.000	0.000	0.000	0.000	0.000	0.227	0.000	0.000	0.000	0.000	0.000	0.000
29 Fish products, E	0.001	0.003	0.000	0.000	0.014	0.000	0.000	0.000	0.000	0.043	0.001	0.001	0.000	0.001	0.000
30 Flour, malt, and starch, E	0.004	0.001	0.000	0.000	0.040	0.099	0.000	0.007	0.000	0.001	0.075	0.013	0.059	0.008	0.002
31 Beet, pulp, and sugar, E	0.000	0.000	0.000	0.001	0.004	0.003	0.000	0.017	0.000	0.000	0.001	0.003	0.000	0.003	0.000
36 Liquor and beer, E	0.000	0.000	0.000	0.000	0.006	0.000	0.000	0.000	0.000	0.000	0.001	0.000	0.039	0.001	0.029
38 Processed foods, M	0.002	0.019	0.003	0.010	0.112	0.069	0.003	0.116	0.000	0.002	0.054	0.058	0.008	0.088	0.011
39 Alcohol and wine, M	0.000	0.000	0.000	0.000	0.000	0.000	0.000	0.000	0.000	0.000	0.000	0.000	0.001	0.000	0.040

1 See note to Table 9.1.

Since the percentage of cost used to purchase resources is large, the percentages left to purchase intermediate goods from the import competing sector and the export sector are correspondingly smaller, and consequently, the indirect effects of tariffs are also smaller. Furthermore, expenditures in the export sector are nearly equal to amounts spent in the import competing sector. The small amount that the Canadian tariff increases the costs of intermediate goods purchased from the import competing sector is about offset by the amount that the US tariff reduces the costs of intermediate goods purchased from the export sector. Except for feed meal (6), the indirect effects of the Canadian and US tariffs, shown in columns 6 and 7 of Table 9.2, do not exceed one per cent of cost. In general, these five producing classifications do not generate antiprotection and are not subject to antiprotection but the tariff and non-tariff protection of resource production is not feasible without protection at the later stages of processing which must absorb the output of the earlier stages.

Both processed tobacco (10) and raw tobacco (81), for example, receive substantial protection in Canada. In the case of raw tobacco (81) the tariff succeeds in blocking imports of cheaper Rhodesian tobacco but South African tobacco may be imported duty free. In the past, production has been located in Ontario where supplies are limited through a system of acreage allotments. About eighty per cent of production is sold to domestic producers of processed tobacco (10). This group is protected by an exceedingly high tariff and receives additional protection with regard to US trade because of the lower price of raw tobacco (81) in Canada. Both the US and Canada support the price of tobacco but it is supported at a higher level in the United States. The cost advantage to Canadian producers in 1961 was about one-third over firms in the US (Trant, MacFarlane, and Fischer, 1968, 21). Since thirty-one per cent of the cost of processed tobacco (10) is used to purchase raw robacco (81), this amounts to a cost advantage of ten per cent. This plus an exceptionally high Canadian tariff gave producers of processed tobacco (10) the amount of protection needed to maintain 1961 levels of tobacco processing in Canada.

The relationship between dairy products (5) and unprocessed milk (74) is similar to the relationship between the two tobacco groups. Production of dairy products (5) is highly protected by the tariff and, in addition, virtually all dairy imports except cheese are embargoed through a system of import licensing. Within Canada prices are supported by offers to purchase and deficiency payments. Fluid milk imports are effectively prohibited by marketing quotas administered at the provincial level. Any relaxation of present levels of protection given to dairy products (5) would create a substantial excess supply of milk.

The situation with regard to feed meal (6) is similar. Largely because of the US price support program, Canadian feed meal (6) producers have had the advantage of low cost wheat (72) (Trant, MacFarlane, and Fischer, 1968, 21). Since feed meal (6) producers use ten per cent of costs to purchase wheat (72) and since wheat (72) has been about one-third cheaper in Canada than in the United States, the Canadian producer has a cost advantage of over three per cent. On the other hand, trade in other grains (73) is less restricted. Of the other grains (73), grain corn, which is imported, is more costly in Canada (Trant, MacFarlane, and Fischer, 1968, 73), but barley and oats are exported from both Canada and the United States.

The simulation indicates that all of these resource absorbing end product classifications were at relatively too high a level in 1961 except processed tobacco (10). These classifications therefore are an exception to the general results discussed in the earlier chapters. The Canadian-US tariff encouraged expansion in the end product classifications and these would decline in free trade. Meat except fish and poultry (3), processed poultry (4), and dairy products (5) operated at a level relatively too high in 1961. Processed tobacco (10) and feed meal (6), however, conform to the behaviour found in the earlier chapters. Processed tobacco (10) is an end product class that would have expanded at free trade prices and feed meal (6) is an intermediate product class that was encouraged, under the tariff, to expand beyond the free trade level.

In four of the five classifications considered in this section, there is a close tie between a producer of end products and one or more of the resource producing groups. Given present world restrictions on agricultural products, the government cannot protect the resource stage of production without also protecting the end product stage. The government's attitude toward protection in this area must, therefore, depend on Canada's comparative advantage in producing the resource.

DOMESTIC INDUSTRIES WITH LESSER RESOURCE DEPENDENCE

The remaining domestic groups in the agriculture and food sector use a lesser percentage of costs to purchase resources. From Table 9.1, column 9, the reader can verify that two per cent of the costs of cereal and bakery (7) producers, eleven per cent of the costs of the sugar refinery products (8) producers, and five per cent of the costs of confectionery products (9) producers are spent on resources. Confectionery products (9) and cereal and bakery products (7) are end product classifications. The former would have increased and the latter would have decreased in 1961 at free trade prices. The sugar refinery products

(8) classification is an intermediate products group which reached a level of production relatively higher than it could have achieved at free trade prices.

Although sugar refinery (8) producers purchase few domestic resources, they make substantial purchases of cane sugar (66) from outside Canada. Domestic resource purchases are obtained from the vegetables (78) classification which accounts for ten per cent of costs. Since almost all of the cane sugar (66) used in Canada in 1961 was imported and since the ratio of imports to production of vegetables (78) is −0.358, the Canadian tariff might have raised the cost of sugar refinery products (8) substantially above the foreign price. The average Canadian tariffs applicable to cane sugar (66) and vegetables (78), however, are low and most sugar is imported under the commonwealth preference rates (Trant, MacFarlane, and Fischer, 1968, 28).

The Canadian tariff schedule with regard to sugar is an exceedingly complicated document designed to encourage processing in Canada at all stages. Canada does not have the resource base required for production of Sugar Refinery Products (8). Production of sugar beets in Canada is supported by deficiency payments to sugar beet producers based on a guaranteed price which is sometimes twice as high as the world price (Trant, MacFarlane, and Fischer, 1968, 29). By attempting, through tariff policy, to establish high cost production in Canada, the government increases the cost of other more efficient industries. Sugar refinery products (8) are important suppliers to the cereal and bakery (7), confectionery products (9), and processed foods (38) producers. Due to an exceedingly high level of tariff protection, imports were equal to only four per cent of output in 1961. It is probable that the Canadian tariff is higher than is necessary to protect this group and that the Canadian price rises above the world price by the largest amount permitted by domestic conditions of supply and demand.

As noted above, confectionery products (9), is one of the end-product groups which, according to the simulation, would be expected to expand in free trade. Considering the relatively high level of direct tariff protection, this is a somewhat surprising outcome. Reductions in the Kennedy Round were quite large. The pre-Kennedy level of antiprotection is 2.5 per cent but this is not a good indication of the total amount of cost distortion present. It includes only the effect of the Canadian tariff as it operates to increase costs of goods purchased from the import competing sector net of the amount that the US tariff reduces costs in the export sector. In free trade the prices of dairy products (5) and of sugar refinery (8) products (which are in the *domestic* sector) would be lower. The simulation takes account of all indirect effects of this type. Although the level of confectionery products (9) output would have expanded under free trade, it would undoubtedly contract if there had been a reduction in direct protection without a simultaneous reduction in the antiprotection.

The Canadian tariff appears to have increased output of the cereal and bakery (7) group above the level which would be attained in free trade. These producers do not benefit directly from lower grain prices in Canada because they make no direct purchase of wheat. The benefits of a Canadian location derive indirectly from the lower prices of flour, malt, and starch (30) but purchases of these products are only ten per cent of cost and this is offset by the seven per cent of cost used to purchase from the processed foods (38) producers who are in the import competing sector. Because the percentage of cost used to purchase from the export sector exceeds the percentage of cost used to purchase from the import competing sector, the Canadian tariff generates only a small amount of anti-protection in the cereal and bakery (7) group. The level of direct protection given to cereal and bakery (7) products was fourteen per cent pre-Kennedy reduced to 11.4 per cent after the Kennedy Round. This is obviously enough to offset the one per cent antiprotection and apparently sufficient to prevent import competition. The ratio of net imports to production is -0.033.

The pre-Kennedy levels of tariffs protecting the cereal and bakery (7) and confectionery products (9) producers appear to be high enough to offset the antiprotection generated by other producer groups such as processed foods (38), dairy products (5), and sugar refinery (8). The sugar refinery (8) producers are important suppliers of intermediate products and a source of antiprotection in several producer classifications.

AGRICULTURAL GROUPS WITH EXPORTABLE OUTPUT

In the export industries as in the agricultural sector generally, there is no clear cut shift toward end product production in the free trade simulation. Liquor and beer (36) is an end product group which expands but this expansion also holds in the case of flour, malt, and starch (30) which specializes at the intermediate product stage. As would be predicted from economic theory, Canadian export industries play the role of exporting Canadian resource products which are relatively abundant. It is also characteristic, in these producer groups, that the level of antiprotection is very low. The fish products (29) producers are an extreme example. The ratio of net exports to output in this group is 0.575. Forty-nine per cent of the costs of fish products (29) are fish landings (89). The level of antiprotection was about 0.5 per cent. With regard to exportable products in general, the Canadian government has the difficult task of demonstrating to the world that Canadian exports are firmly based on the Canadian comparative advantage and that it is to the interest of Canada and the rest of the world that these goods should be exchanged for goods which Canada produces at relatively high cost.

The Canadian comparative advantage in production of flour, malt, and starch (30) is based on her comparative advantage in wheat production. Fifteen per cent of Canada's production of flour, malt, and starch (30) is exported. These producers use twenty-five per cent of their expenditures to purchase wheat (72). Since high quality wheat is available at low cost, a Canadian location is of considerable advantage. It has been estimated that the US price support program has raised the cost of wheat to the US producer by enough to give Canadian flour millers an eighteen per cent cost advantage (Wonnacott and Wonnacott, 1967, 265). Exports of the flour, malt, and starch (30) producers are predominantly wheat flour which is subject to a US quota under section 22 of the Agriculture Adjustment Act. This US quota is of little significance, however, because the United States is also a wheat exporting nation.

The Canadian comparative advantage in liquor and beer (36) is in some part due to the malting quality of Canadian barley. Canadian barley, however, can be and is, in fact, purchased by producers located outside Canada. Liquor and beer (36) producers use only 3.1 per cent of costs to purchase other grain (73) and expenditures on wheat (72) are negligible. Purchases of grain are made indirectly through the flour, malt, and starch (30) classification which accounts for six per cent of costs. Value added in liquor and beer (36) is nearly one-half of costs. Although product differentiation among the liquor and beer (36) producers opens broad opportunities for two-way trade, Canada was overwhelmingly an exporter of these products in 1964. The simulation indicates that expanded production of liquor and beer (36) would have moved Canada closer to her 1961 comparative advantage.

The average pre-Kennedy tariff rate of forty-four per cent for liquor and beer (36) was exceptionally high. This was, no doubt, motivated by a desire to create a Canadian preference for the home product in an area where product differentiation is important. It is most probable, however, that the amount of protection given was more than the amount needed. Kennedy Round reductions in the Canadian tariff were substantial. Like many products in the agriculture and foods sector, Canadian liquor and beer producers are protected by provincial regulations which establish various kinds of non-tariff barriers (see Stegeman, 1973, 65-75).

Production of beet, pulp, and sugar (31) plays no essential role in resource use nor is it among the industries operating at too low a level in 1961. According to the simulation it would not have been possible for Canada to maintain its 1961 level of beet, pulp, and sugar (31) production if resource costs had been based on free trade prices. The 1961 level of protection at the resource stage was maintained by a system of deficiency payments which, as noted above, provided returns to growers well above the prices normally paid by the beet, pulp, and sugar (31) producers. The beet, pulp, and sugar (31) producer group is quantitatively small. Although minute amounts of beet pulp are exported to the US, none was imported in 1964. Exports of this group (but not production) are dominated by exports of products made from maple sugar in which Canada does have a comparative advantage. Although the simulation indicates that 1961 production of beet, pulp, and sugar (31) would decline under free trade pricing, it must be assumed that this decline would not extend to production of maple products.

Kennedy Round tariff reductions in all the four export groups were large compared to reductions elsewhere in the agriculture and food sector. The data indicate that these reductions had little economic impact, however. Antiprotection in the agricultural export sector is low. The simulation implies that all except the beet, pulp, and sugar (31) producers would have expanded under free trade pricing.

IMPORT COMPETING AGRICULTURE AND FOOD INDUSTRIES

The two import competing groups in the agriculture and food sector are processed foods (38) and alcohol and wine (39). Processed foods (38) is the larger, and alcohol and wine (39) is the smaller producer group in this sector. In both, purchases of resource commodities are a moderate percentage of cost.

The circumstances facing alcohol and wine (39) producers are quite different from those facing the liquor and beer (36) producers discussed above. The value of liquor and beer (36) production is considerably the larger and only 3.3 per cent of costs of liquor and beer (36) production is used to purchase from the resource industries. Purchases from the export sector exceed purchases from the import competing sector. The value of alcohol and wine (39) production, on the other hand, is quite small. Significant purchases are made from the resource sector and purchases from the import sector exceed the value of purchases from the export sector. Purchases of the resource commodities consist largely of purchases of nuts, fruits, and berries (77) which account for about twelve per cent of costs.

Processed foods (38) producers use nearly sixteen per cent of costs to purchase resources. These producers are heavily dependent on the import sector which accounts for perhaps one-fourth of cost. Despite the concentration of purchases in the resource and import sectors, no single classification of industries predominates as a supplier to the processed foods (38) producers. Purchases are spread over a large number of classifications. Sales are also dispersed but, as is clear from Table 4.3, such sales constitute a significant portion of costs in a number of other producer classifications.

As the name suggests, processed foods (38) producers supply a wide range of intermediate services including dehydrating, concentrating, canning, freezing, and cooking. A portion of this group has been studied in detail by Eastman and Stykolt (1967, 111-48) who found that economies of scale are possible with regard to many of these activities and that the industry failed, on the whole, to reach the size necessary to benefit from economies of scale. Since the processed food group is an important supplier of intermediate goods, the failure to achieve the lowest unit cost must adversely affect the performance of other groups in the economy. The pre-Kennedy level of antiprotection of four per cent is the highest of all the agriculture and food groups. Even after the Kennedy Round, the cost of intermediate goods were higher by 3.6 per cent due to the indirect effect of the Canadian tariff. Net protection after the Kennedy Round was brought down to an average of 5.5 per cent.

The average tariff on alcohol and wine (39) is about thirteen per cent pre-Kennedy, offset by about two per cent antiprotection. The average duty on alcohol and wine (39) actually increased after the Kennedy Round. This is because the pre-Kennedy tariff reflected the situation as it was in 1961. Increases in the tariff after 1965 but before the end of the Kennedy Round negotiations increased the average tariff for this group. The Kennedy Round reduced the tariff but it remained higher than the 1961 level. The anti-protection for the alcohol and wine (39) group overstates the amount that the Canadian tariff increases the costs of intermediate goods. Sugar for use in the manufacture of wine enters under the low rate permitted by tariff item 13405-1 and raw sugar imported for production of refined sugar to be used in the manufacture of wine is subject to a 99 per cent drawback. It would be a mistake, however, to make too much of this point. Sugar purchases are only 3.2 per cent of the cost of alcohol and wine (39). The simulation indicates that under conditions of free trade, the level of 1961 production in alcohol and wine (39) would have expanded. An increase in the output of alcohol and wine (39) would have moved Canada in the direction of its comparative advantage yet these producers depended on the 1961 Canadian tariff for protection because of the high levels of anti-protection present.

CONCLUSIONS

The descriptive tables in this chapter point to several features of the agriculture and food sector which might have some bearing on future trade negotiations.

1. According to the simulation, the sugar refinery products (8) industry and the beet, pulp, and sugar (31) industry were expanded beyond the level required by comparative advantage. It is not possible to establish comparative advantage in these groups on the basis of resource abundance in Canada because both industries depend on imported cane sugar or on Canadian sugar beet production which was heavily subsidized in 1961. The product flows of Table 9.3 indicate that these producers are important suppliers to cereal and bakery (7), confectionery products (9), and processed foods (38). The Kennedy Round reduction on beet, pulp, and sugar (31) was notable but the reduction applying to sugar refinery products (8) was modest.

2. Processed foods (38) is also an important supplier of intermediate goods. Since it is also import competing it may be anticipated that many of these producers will price up to the Canadian tariff. It is therefore probable that a significant amount of antiprotection is generated. Kennedy Round reductions were above the average for the sector as a whole. Since there is evidence that economies of scale are possible in some lines, a greater degree of specialization would be expected under free trade. However, the simulation indicates that production in 1961 exceeded the level expected under free trade and therefore under free trade a decline in the Canadian share of this production is probable.

3. According to the simulation, the feed meal and flour (6) classification and the liquor and beer (36) classification failed to reach the level optimal for comparative advantage in 1961. Resource statistics indicate that comparative advantage is based in part on Canadian grain production. Substantial Kennedy Round cuts were made in the Canadian tariffs which apply in these two categories but, given Provincial restrictions on the sales of Liquor and Beer (36) and given Canada's comparative advantage in grain, reductions are not likely to lead to increased import competition.

4. The alcohol and wine (39) and the processed tobacco (10) classifications are end product producers which operated at a level relatively too low for comparative advantage in 1961. Each group is identified with a particular resource product. The Canadian tariff and other non-tariff barriers in Canada were significant in maintaining 1961 levels of output. The US tariff is of correspondingly less importance. If it is desired to expand production without increasing direct protection, it must be achieved through reduced antiprotection.

5. In the agricultural sector effort to protect both resource production and end product production was not uniformly successful in 1961. Production of alcohol and wine (39), liquor and beer (36), confectionary products (9), and processed tobacco (10) would have expanded at free trade prices.

Notes

PREFACE

1 The seminal article was Barber (1955).
2 An excellent critical summary of the effective tariff literature can be found
   in Grubel (1971). See also Balassa (1971) for a statement on the merits of
   the theory of effective protection. A comprehensive bibliography is found
   in Grubel and Johnson (1971).
3 For a survey see Chipman (1965). Recent examples of empirical work are
   Werin (1965); Bruno (1966); Lage (1970); and Evans (1974).

CHAPTER 1

1 See example, McKenzie (1954), Jones (1961), and other works cited in
   J.S. Chipman (1965).
2 See for example Werin (1965), Bruno (1966), and Evans (1972).
3 For simplicity, it is assumed in this example that we are considering the
   long run in which there are no fixed costs.
4 We must always bear in mind, of course, that individual firms within each
   industry may differ from the pattern predicted for the industry.
5 Factor intensity reversals occur when relative factor intensities are not
   uniquely determined by relative factor prices. See Pearce (1952) and
   Johnson (1957).
6 See W.W. Leontief (1964), Yahr (1968), Philpot (1970), and Ball (1970).
7 See Young (1957, 59), Melvin and Wilkinson (1968), and Wilkinson and
   Norrie (1976) for example.
8 The following quotation is found in Eastman and Stykolt (1967, 15).
   'Foreign tariffs inhibit international trade by requiring a price in the

potentially exporting country lower by at least the amount of the tariff than would otherwise obtain. The Canadian tariff permits prices higher by the amount of the relevant rate of duty to be set in Canada without stimulating imports.' This is effectively a verbal summary of the inequalities discussed below.

9 We should also like to argue that resources are inelastic in supply because fixed costs are a large proportion of total cost. The question of elasticity must depend on the time period considered and it is almost certain that there would be exceptions to any generalization applied to such a large number of resources. The question pertinent in the present context is whether or not supply will respond to the general equilibrium changes considered in a model in which all prices are allowed to vary. This is an empirical question which is nearly impossible to answer because history provides too few experiments of this kind for us to observe.

10 For an example of analysis based on this type of classification See (Meade, 1951, chap. 28).

11 Non-tariff barriers have been the subject of much research in the last few years and a considerable volume of literature is available. Readers interested in Canadian non-tariff barriers are referred to Grey (1973), Pestieau and Henry (1972), and Stegeman (1973).

12 See Johnson (1972, 338). In some cases it is possible to extend the discriminant analysis further in the direction of hypothesis testing. However, in the case under consideration, it is clear that the data cannot satisfy the stochastic assumptions required in such analysis. It should be noted, however, that the hypothesis tested below is non-parametric and hence does not depend on the stochastic assumptions to which we allude.

13 For a review of the literature on this topic see Economic Council of Canada (1975, chapter 6).

CHAPTER 2

1 See appendix, p. 54 for list of notation.

2 See Gale (1961, 10, theorem 1.1, and 82, theorem 3.2).

3 The proof in this section is a linear programming version of Samuelson's (1939) theorem on the gains from trade. See also Kemp (1962) and Samuelson (1962).

CHAPTER 3

1 These cards contain the same information as is available in Statistics Canada (12-527, various).

2 The coefficients in Table 2.2 are defined in normal units of quantity. Those in Table 3.4 strictly speaking are in value units. Therefore, the two tables are the same only if we define units of quantity as the amount that can be purchased for one dollar in 1961.

CHAPTER 4

1 Only thirty-nine per cent of output is delivered to the other producers as intermediate product. Most output is classified as capital investment which is part of final demand. It may be assumed that most of this will be used as intermediate product in future time periods.
2 See, for example, tariff items 40900-1 through 42605-1, as they existed prior to the Kennedy Round. Provisions of this type are scattered through-out the 1965 tariff schedule and others can be found in schedule B where goods subject to drawback are listed.

CHAPTER 5

1 Production of cement, for example, is possible in most regions in Canada. See Eastman and Stykolt (1967, 157).
2 In the late fifties a patent pooling company called Canadian Radio Patents Limited came in for public criticism because it used patents to block imports of foreign made television and radio sets. See Masson and Whitely (1960, 36).

CHAPTER 6

1 Since the time of writing, changes in the US copyright law have removed this restriction. See US *Code Congressional and Administrative News* (1976, 6210-7).

CHAPTER 9

1 The eastern Canadian cane sugar refiners were fined under conspiracy charges in 1963 and in 1969 the Tariff Board was requested to make an inquiry (Federal Task Force on Agriculture, 1970, 246).

Bibliography

ANDERSON, JAMES E. (1970) 'General equilibrium and the effective rate of protection.' *Journal of Political Economy* 78, 717-24
- and Seiji Naya (1969) 'Substitution and two concepts of effective rate of protection.' *American Economic Review* 49, 607-12

BHAGWATI, JAGDISH N. and T. N. SRINIVASAN (1973) 'The general equilibrium theory of effective protection and resource allocation.' *Journal of International Economics* 3, 259-81

BALASSA, BELA (1965) 'Tariff protection in industrial countries: an evaluation.' *Journal of Political Economy* 73, 573-94
- (1971) 'Effective protection: a summary appraisal.' In Herbert G. Grubel and Harry G. Johnson, eds., *Effective Tariff Protection.* Geneva; General Agreement on Tariffs and Trade, 247-60
- and DANIEL M. SCHYDLOWSKY (1968) 'Effective tariffs, domestic cost of foreign exchange, and the equilibrium exchange rate.' *Journal of Political Economy* 76, 348-60
- STEPHEN E. GUISINGER, and DANIEL M. SCHYDLOWSKY (1970) 'The effective rates of protection and the question of labor protection in the United States: a comment.' *Journal of Political Economy* 78, 1150-62

BALL, D.S. (1970) 'Factor Intensity reversals in international comparisons of factor costs and factor use.' *Journal of Political Economy* 74, 77-80

BARBER, CLARENCE L. (1955) 'Canadian tariff policy.' *Canadian Journal of Economics and Political Science* 21, 513-30

BARDHAN, V. PRANAB (1965) 'International differences in production functions, trade and factor prices.' *Economic Journal* 75, 81-7

BASEVI, GIORGIO (1966) 'The United States tariff structure: estimates of effective rates of protection of United States industries and industrial labor.' *Review of Economics and Statistics* 48, 147-60

BATRA, RAVEENDRA N. and FRANCISCO R. CASAS (1974) 'Traded and non-traded intermediate inputs, real wages, and resource allocation.' *Canadian Journal of Economics* 7, 225-39

BEIGIE, CARL E. (1970) THE CANADIAN-US AUTOMOBILE AGREEMENT: AN EVALUATION. Montreal, The National Planning Association of the United States and the Private Planning Association of Canada

BERGLAS, EITAN and ASSAF RAZIN (1973) 'Effective protection and decreasing returns to scale.' *American Economic Review* 63, 733-7

BOND, DAVID E. and RONALD J. WONNACOTT (1968) *Trade Liberalization and the Canadian Furniture Industry.* Toronto, University of Toronto Press

BRUNO, MICHAEL (1966) 'A programming model for Israel.' In Irma Adelman and Erik Thorbecke, eds., *The Theory and Design of Economic Development.* Baltimore, Johns Hopkins Press, 327-54

– (1967) 'Optimal patterns of trade and development.' *Review of Economics and Statistics* 49, 545-54

– (1973) 'Protection and tariff change under general equilibrium.' *Journal of International Economics* 3, 205-25

CASAS, FRANCISCO R. (1973) 'Optimal effective protection in general equilibrium.' *American Economic Review* 63, 714-16

CHANG, WINSTON W. and WOLFGANG MAYER (1973) 'Intermediate goods in a general equilibrium trade model.' *International Economic Review* 14, 447-59

CHIPMAN, JOHN S. (1965) 'A survey of the theory of international trade: part 3, the modern theory.' *Econometrica* 34, 18-76

COMMITTEE FOR ECONOMIC DEVELOPMENT (1963) *Comparative Tariffs and Trade: The United States and the European Common Market.* Supplementary Paper Number 14, prepared by Frances K. Topping (New York)

CORDEN, W.M. (1966) 'The structure of a tariff system and the effective protective rate.' *Journal of Political Economy* 74, 221-37

– (1969) 'Effective protective rates in the general equilibrium model: a geometric note.' *Oxford Economic Papers* 21, 135-41

– (1971a) 'The substitution problem in the theory of effective protection.' *Journal of International Economics* 1, 37-57

– (1971b) *The Theory of Protection.* Oxford, Clarendon Press

DEPARTMENT OF TRADE AND COMMERCE (1967) 'Tariff concessions granted by Canada.' *Foreign Trade* 128, 39-42

DORNBUSCH, RUDIGER (1974) 'Tariffs and non-traded goods.' *Journal of International Economics* 4, 177-85

EASTMAN, HARRY C. and STEFAN STYKOLT (1967) *The Tariff and Competition in Canada.* Toronto, Macmillan

ECONOMIC COUNCIL OF CANADA (1967) *Fourth Annual Review. The Canadian Economy for the 1960's to the 1970's.* Ottawa, Queen's Printer
- (1975) *Looking Outward: A New Trade Strategy for Canada.* Ottawa, Information Canada
ETHIER, WILFRED J. (1971) 'General equilibrium theory and the concept of the effective rate of protection.' In Herbert Grubel and Harry G. Johnson, eds., *Effective Tariff Protection.* Geneva, General Agreement on Tariffs and Trade, 17-36
- (1972) 'Input substitution and the concept of the effective rate of protection.' *Journal of Political Economy* 80, 34-47
EVANS, HENRY DAVID (1970) 'A programming model of trade and protection.' In I.A. McDougall and R.H. Snape, eds., *Studies in International Economics.* Amsterdam, North-Holland Publishing Company, 19-33
- (1971) 'Effects of protection in a general equilibrium framework.' *Review of Economics and Statistics* 53, 147-56
- (1972) *A General Equilibrium Analysis of Protection: the Effects of Protection in Australia.* Amsterdam, North-Holland Publishing Company
FEDERAL TASK FORCE ON AGRICULTURE (1969) Report: *Canadian Agriculture in the Seventies*
FINGER, J.M. (1969) 'Substitution and the effective rate of protection.' *Journal of Political Economy* 77, 972-5
GALE, DAVID (1960) *The Theory of Linear Economic Models.* New York, McGraw-Hill Book Company
GREY, RODNEY DE C. (1973) *The Development of the Canadian Anti-Dumping System.* Montreal, Private Planning Association
GRUBEL HERBERT G. (1971) 'Effective tariff protection: a non-specialist guide to the theory, policy implications and controversies.' In Herbert G. Grubel and Harry G. Johnson, eds., *Effective Tariff Protection.* Geneva, General Agreement on Tariffs and Trade, 1-15
- and HARRY G. JOHNSON, eds. (1971) *Effective Tariff Protection.* Geneva, General Agreement on Tariffs and Trade
- and P.J. LLOYD (1971) 'Factor substitution and effective tariff rates.' *Review of Economic Studies* 38, 95-103
GUISINGER, STEPHEN E. (1969) 'Negative value added and the theory of effective protection.' *Quarterly Journal of Economics* 83, 415-33
HANSEN, BENT (1974) 'Effective protection – a probabilistic argument.' *Journal of International Economics* 4, 207-11
HAVILAND, W.E., N.S. TAKACSY, and E.M. CAPE (1968) *Trade Liberalization and the Canadian Pulp and Paper Industry.* Toronto, University of Toronto Press

HUMPHREY, DAVID B. (1969) 'Measuring the effective rate of protection: direct and indirect effects.' *Journal of Political Economy* 77, 834-44
- and T. TSUKAHARA JR. (1970) 'On substitution and the effective rate of protection.' *International Economic Review* 11, 488-96
JOHNSON, HARRY G. (1957) 'Factor endowments, international trade and factor prices.' *Manchester School of Economic and Social Studies* 25, 270-83
- (1960) 'The cost of protection and the scientific tariff.' *Journal of Political Economy* 58, 327-45
- (1965) 'The theory of tariff structure with special reference to world trade and development.' *Trade and Development* (Geneva: L'institut Universitaire de Hautes Etudes Internationales) 9-28
- (1969) 'The theory of effective protection and preferences.' *Economica* 36, 119-38
JOHNSON, J. (1972) *Econometric Methods*, 2nd ed. New York, McGraw-Hill Book Company
JONES, RONALD W. (1961) 'Comparative advantage and the theory of tariffs: a multi-country multi-commodity model.' *Review of Economic Studies* 28, 161-75
- (1971) 'Effective protection and substitution.' *Journal of International Economics* 1, 59-81
KEMP, MURRAY C. (1962) 'The gains from international trade.' *Economic Journal* 72, 803-19
- (1969) *A Contribution to the General Equilibrium Theory of Preferential Trading.* Amsterdam, North-Holland Publishing Company
KOOPMANS, TJALLING C., ed. (1951) *Activity Analysis of Production and Allocation. New York, John Wiley*
LAGE, GERALD M. (1970) 'A linear programming analysis of tariff protection.' *Western Economic Journal* 8, 167-85
LEITH, J. CLARK (1968a) 'Across-the-board nominal tariff changes and the effective rate of protection.' *Economic Journal* 78, 982-84
- (1968b) 'Substitution and supply elasticities in calculating the effective protective rate.' *Quarterly Journal of Economics* 82, 588-601
- 'The effect of tariffs on production, consumption and trade: a revised analysis.' *American Economic Review* 61, 74-81
- and G.L. REUBER (1969) 'The impact of the industrial countries' tariff structure on their imports of manufactures from less-developed areas: a comment.' *Economica* 36, 75-80
LEONTIEF, WASSILY (1964) 'International factor costs and factor use.' *American Economic Review* 54, 335-45

LERMER, GEORGE (1973) 'Evidence from trade data regarding the rationalizing of Canadian industry.' *Canadian Journal of Economics* 6, 248-56

MCDOUGALL, I.A. (1970) 'Non-traded commodities and the pure theory of international trade.' In I.A. McDougall and R.H. Snape, eds., *Studies in International Economics*. Amsterdam, North-Holland Publishing Company, 157-92

MCKENZIE, LIONEL W. (1954) 'Specialisation and efficiency in world production.' *Review of Economic Studies* 21, 165-80

MCKINNON, RONALD I. (1966) 'Intermediate products and differential tariffs: a generalization of Lerner's symmetry theorem.' *Quarterly Journal of Economics* 80, 584-615

MAITI, PRADIP (1973) 'Factor price equalization theorem in linear programming.' *Journal of International Economics* 3, 367-78

MASSELL, B.F. (1968) 'The resource-allocative effects of a tariff and the effective protection of individual inputs.' *Economic Record* 44, 369-76

MASSON, FRANCIS and H. EDWARD ENGLISH (1963) *Invisible Trade Barriers Between Canada and the United States.* Montreal, National Planning Association of the United States and the Private Planning Association of Canada

MASSON, FRANCIS and J.B. WHITELY (1960) *Barriers to Trade Between Canada and the United States.* Montreal, Canadian American Committee

MAYER, WOLFGANG (1971) 'Effective tariff protection in a simple general equilibrium model.' *Economica* 38, 253-68

MEADE, J.E. (1951) *The Balance of Payments.* London, Oxford University Press

MELVIN, JAMES R. (1970) 'Commodity taxation as a determinant of trade.' *Canadian Journal of Economics* 3, 62-78

– (1975) *The Tax Structure and Canadian Trade: A Theoretical Analysis.* Ottawa, Information Canada

– and BRUCE W. WILKINSON (1968) *Effective Protection in the Canadian Economy.* Ottawa, Information Canada

MICHAELY, MICHAEL (1975) 'The welfare loss of negative value-added.' *Journal of International Economics* 5, 283-87

MINHAS, BAGICHA SINGH (1963) *An International Comparison of Factor Cost and Factor Use.* Amsterdam, North-Holland Publishing Company

NORMAN, N.R. (1975) 'On the relationship between prices of home-produced and foreign commodities.' *Oxford Economic Papers* 27, 426-39

PEARCE, I.F. (1952) 'The Factor price equalization myth.' *Review of Economic Studies* 19, 111-9

PESTIEAU, CAROLINE and JACQUES HENRY (1972) *Non-Tariff Barriers as a Problem in International Development.* Private Planning Association of Canada

PHILPOT, GORDON (1970) 'Labour quality, returns to scale and elasticity of factor substitution.' *Review of Economic Statistics* 52, 194-9

POSTNER, HARRY H., assisted by DON GILFIX (1975) *Factor Content of Canadian International Trade: An Input-Output Analysis.* Economic Council of Canada

PRESS, S. JAMES (1973) *Applied Multivariate Analysis.* Chicago, Holt, Rinehart and Winston

RAMASWAMI, V.K. and T.N. SRINIVASAN (1971) 'Tariff structure and resource allocation in the presence of factor substitution.' In J. Bhagwati, R.W. Jones, R.A. Mundell, and J. Vanek, eds., *Trade, Balance of Payments and Growth, Papers in honour of Charles P. Kindleberger.* Amsterdam, North-Holland Publishing Company

RAY, ALOK (1973) 'Non-traded inputs and effective protection: a general equilibrium analysis.' *Journal of International Economics* 3, 245-57

ROBINSON, JOAN (1941) 'Rising supply price.' *Economica* n.s. 8, 1-8

RUFFIN, ROY J. (1969) 'Tariffs, intermediate goods, and domestic protection.' *American Economic Review* 59, 261-9

- (1971) 'The welfare implications of effective protection.' In Herbert G. Grubel and Harry G. Johnson, eds., *Effective Tariff Protection.* Geneva, General Agreement on Tariffs and Trade, 85-105

SAMUELSON, PAUL A. (1939) 'The gains from international trade.' *Canadian Journal of Economics and Political Science* 5, 195-205

- (1953-4) 'Prices of factors and goods in general equilibrium.' *Review of Economic Studies* 21, 1-20

- (1962) 'The gains from international trade once again' *Economic Journal* 72, 820-9

SCHEFFMAN, D.T. (1973) 'Some remarks on the net production possibilities set in models with intermediate goods.' *Journal of International Economics* 3, 291-5

SCHWEINBERGER, A.G. (1975) 'Non-traded intermediate products and the measurement of protection.' *Oxford Economic Papers* 27, 215-31

SENDO, YOSHIKI (1974) 'The theory of effective protection in general equilibrium; an extension of the Bhagwati-Srinivasan analysis.' *Journal of International Economics* 4, 213-15

SHOVEN, JOHN B. and JOHN WHALLEY (1974) 'On the computation of competitive equilibrium on international markets with tariffs.' *Journal of International Economics* 4, 341-54

STAELIN, CHARLES P. (1976) 'A general-equilibrium model of tariffs in a noncompetitive economy.' *Journal of International Economics* 6, 39-63

STATISTICS CANADA (65-004, 1965) *Trade of Canada Exports: Calendar Years, December 1964.* Ottawa, Information Canada

- (65-007, 1965) *Trade of Canada Imports by Commodities, December 1964.* Ottawa, Information Canada
- (15-501, 1969) *The Input-Output Structure of the Canadian Economy, 1961* 1. Ottawa, Information Canada
- (65-203, 1969) *Trade of Canada Imports Calendar Years, 1960-1962.* Ottawa, Information Canada
- (12-527, various) *Convertibility Index of Customs Tariff Items to the Import Commodity Classification.* Ottawa, Information Canada

STEGEMAN, KLAUS (1973) *Canadian Non-Tariff Barriers to Trade.* Montreal, Private Planning Association

TAN, AUGUSTINE H.H. (1970) 'Differential tariffs, negative value-added and the theory of effective protection.' *American Economic Review* 60, 107-16

TAYLOR, LANCE and STEPHEN L. BLACK (1974) 'Practical general equilibrium estimation of resource pulls under trade liberalization.' *Journal of International Economics* 4, 37-58

TRANT, GERALD I., DAVID L. MACFARLANE, and LEWIS A. FISCHER (1968) *Trade Liberalization and Canadian Agriculture.* Toronto, University of Toronto Press

TRAVIS, WILLIAM P. (1964) *The Theory of Trade and Protection.* Cambridge, Mass., Harvard University Press
- (1968) 'The effective rate of protection and the question of labor protection in the United States.' *Journal of Political Economy* 76, 443-61
- (1972) 'Production, trade and protection when there are many commodities and two factors.' *American Economic Review* 62, 87-106

US Code Congressional and Administrative News, 13 (1976) 'General revision of the copyright law.' St Paul, Minnesota, West Publishing Company

WEISER, LAWRENCE A. (1968) 'Changing factor requirements of United States foreign trade.' *Review of Economics and Statistics* 50, 356-60

WERIN, LARS (1965) *A Study of Production, Trade and Resource Allocation.* Stockholm, Almquist and Wiksell

WILKINSON, B.W. and K. NORRIE (1976) *Effective Protection and the Return to Capital.* Ottawa, information Canada

WILLIAMS, JAMES R. (1972a) 'Effects of a customs union on the welfare of a joining nation.' *Canadian Journal of Economics* 5, 131-7
- (1972b) 'Customs unions: a welfare criterion for the general case.' *Manchester School* 40, 385-96
- (1975) *Resources, Tariffs, and Trade: Ontario's Stake.* Toronto, University of Toronto Press

WONNACOTT, RONALD J. (1975) *Canada's Trade Options.* Ottawa, Information Canada

- and PAUL WONNACOTT (1967) *Free Trade Between the United States and Canada: The Potential Economic Effects.* Cambridge, Mass., Harvard University Press

YAHR, MERLE I. (1968) 'Human capital and factor substitution in the CES production function.' In Peter B. Kenen and Roger Lawrence, eds., *The Open Economy: Essays on International Trade and Finance.* New York, Columbia University Press

YOUNG, J. (1957) *Canadian Commercial Policy.* Ottawa, Royal Commission on Canada's Economic Prospects

Index

DATE DUE